CONTENTS

iii

PREACHING
AT THE PARISH
COMMUNION

Series 3—YEAR TWO GOSPELS

Hugh Fearn

MOWBRAYS
LONDON & OXFORD

© *A. R. Mowbray & Co Ltd 1973*

ISBN 0 264 64612 6

First published in 1973
by A. R. Mowbray & Co Ltd
The Alden Press, Osney Mead,
Oxford, OX2 oEG

Text set in 12/13 pt. Monotype Bembo, printed by letterpress,
and bound in Great Britain at The Pitman Press, Bath

*The readings for the five Sundays before Advent Sunday are always to be those provided for Trininty 23 and the four weeks following. Readings for Trinity 18 to Trinity 22 will be used according as they are needed.

INTRODUCTION

THE VITALITY and impact of any sermon, empowered by the Holy Spirit, depends upon the preacher, those who have come to hear and the message that is proclaimed. The aim should always be to evoke a response. This cannot be achieved unless due weight is given to these three related factors in every sermon situation.

THE PREACHER

There is a sense in which it will always be the gospel according to the individual preacher; heretical or otherwise. That which a preacher proclaims is the outcome of his own understanding and knowledge of the faith. It follows that a preacher must be a man of God committed to the study of scripture and theology and utterly dependent upon God in prayer. These are universal conditions for all preachers; but there is another variable individual quality which comprises the specific gifts which God has given to each preacher. 'Know thyself' is pertinent to a preaching ministry; our limitations as well as our strong points. Preaching is essentially a personal art; although we seek not to attract a personal following but to direct men and women to follow Christ. How we perform in the pulpit must be in accord with ourselves, we cannot get away with not being ourselves using either words or actions which are not appropriate to *me* as a person. That is why we cannot preach a sermon of another. This does not mean that the sermon outlines in this book cannot be profitably used by others; if the reverse were true I should not have spent time composing them, nor my publishers printing them. We can draw on the ideas of others, but in using them they must be clothed with the *person* (that is the word, not personality) of the particular preacher. Any preacher will develop and adapt his style over the years and in composing and delivering each sermon he needs to be mindful of the particular occasion on which the sermon is to be preached. That means that he needs to remember those who will come to hear and from whom there should be a response.

A preaching ministry is moulded in part by those who have come to hear. Most of our preaching, and certainly at the Parish Communion, will be to men, women and children committed to Christ. The depth of their Christian commitment and its needs can be known only to the preacher through his pastoral contact and concern for the people to whom he ministers. In terms of awareness of our hearers it is well to remember that there are many concerns which are felt and experienced in common and that few of us are uninfluenced by current events brought into our lives by modern means of communication. Nevertheless it is well to remember that when we are preaching to few or to many we are preaching to each individual hearer. If we ask the question, 'What have they come to hear?' can we not best answer this by saying 'How to live out my Christian commitment in a contemporary world'. This means that we must make our preaching relevant, as Jesus made his preaching relevant. This does not mean that topicality has a prior claim; it means that we try to relate the gospel truths to the present needs, fears and aspirations of those who have come to hear.

THE MESSAGE

It is important that every sermon should be expressive of the essential Christian *kerygma*. Each gospel incident, parable or saying of Jesus must be seen against the mighty act of God in Christ crucified, risen and ascended; the means of our redemption. The depths of this are explored in the variety of the entirety of the Christian faith as summarised in the Creed and undergirded by the evidence of the scriptures as we proceed through the calendar year of the eucharistic readings. The outline sermons in this volume are based on the gospels for Year Two of the Series 3 Communion Service. A few of them have been preached in my church during 1972. All have been read by Canon William Purcell of Worcester Cathedral and I am again grateful to him for helpful comments on the original drafts; though I accept personal responsibility for them all as they now appear in print. Again I am indebted to my publishers, Messrs A. R. Mowbray & Co. Ltd, and in particular wish to thank Mr John Stockdale for his personal assistance in bringing this book to its final publication stage. Engagement in active parochial ministry, with commitments to Readers in the Diocese of London and nationally, means that in the writing of this volume I have made a further encroachment upon time which ought to have been given to my family. My thanks are particularly due to my wife for her constant support and encouragement in all that I undertake. Mrs Dorothy Ickinger has typed the final manuscript and again the Reverend Wilfred Beale has helped in the final product.

Hugh Fearn

Northwood,
St Chad, 1973.

FOURTH SUNDAY BEFORE CHRISTMAS

Down to earth

> St Matthew 25.36 (NEB). *'When in prison you visited me.'*

INTRODUCTION

This parable of the heavenly judgement has an unexpected down-to-earth texture. The questions asked are not 'What do you believe?' but 'How did you act?' Even those selected for heavenly reward were taken aback and asked, 'Lord, when was it that we saw you hungry and fed you, or thirsty and gave you drink, a stranger and took you home, or naked and clothed you? When did we see you ill or in prison, and come to visit you?' (St Matthew 25.37–39). Belief is important, but people more so; we must act on our Christian commitment to enable more and more men and women to become mature and what God intended them to be. But who are Christ's brothers? Many commentators on this passage consider the caring responsibility to be expressed within the Christian community. Not so Michael Quoist; in *Christ is Alive*, he argues that as God is the Father of all, our responsibility as Christians is to enable all men and women to reach their potential and become mature in Christ. Whichever view we accept, we must admit that the sphere of concern is far wider than that which applied in the first century for the early Christians. Our aim should surely be to care for those we encounter in life's journey at home, at work and in our leisure associations be it church or club. As we offer this care, not with any selfish aim of an assured place in heaven, we should only be aware of an outpouring of love—our love, Christ's love, God's love.

APPLICATION

Few of us have the opportunity of visiting men and women in prison. But these words *in prison* take on a wider and deeper significance if we extend their meaning to cover an aspect of

5

contemporary society, *imprisonment*. We shall find that most people today are imprisoned in one way or another; man may have come of age and be technically advanced, but in terms of living he is still immature. Two areas of imprisonment in the twentieth century serve to show the kind of *visiting* which is necessary.

(1) *Home imprisonment*

This can take several forms. Illness or limited mobility in old age may enforce confinement, but such people need life and love taking them. Hundreds in bed-sits, high-rise flats are lonely. Thousands living on their own—widows with only memories for company, wives with children off their hands and husbands out most of the day; these need to be brought into the life of the local community. But is there a local community? Should not the church be the focus of community-centredness? The problem is that many people imprisoned in their homes do not recognise their imprisonment.

(2) *Job imprisonment*

Again this can take many forms. Perhaps its worst manifestation is the monotony in the routine of work on a conveyor-belt. Yet, at the other extreme, there is the confident business executive, highly salaried with many material possessions; his job can imprison him giving him little time for his home and family, and making real friends as distinct from business acquaintances. Increasingly job imprisonment will take the form of redundancy and being declared of no use to society. Should not the Christian bring *life* to such people?

These two categories by no means exhaust contemporary styles of imprisonment, where the only release can come through Christ. Too often Christians have set their eyes on heaven and forgotten the earth, which is God's world where all men can be co-creators. God did not (does not) ignore it, he came down to earth.

THIRD SUNDAY BEFORE CHRISTMAS

Prophecy fulfilled

> St Luke 4.21 (JB). *'This text is being fulfilled today even* as you listen.'

INTRODUCTION

Galilee was unusually excited that particular day. The noise and bustle of everyday activity had given place to noise of eager and chattering people awaiting an event with anticipation. Most people were determined to be in the synagogue that morning, aiming to get there early in order to secure an advantageous position. The enthusiasm was intense and all because the local boy had returned home and they were anxious to hear him preach. There was no doubt in their minds that he would be invited to give the sermon that sabbath morning. What would he say? They had already heard of his reputation elsewhere.

The service began with the customary prayers. Then came a reading from the Law. The President then invited Jesus to read the lection from the Prophets, which carried with it the responsibility to expound the passage. Jesus accepted the invitation and stood to read the lesson; then, as custom demanded, he sat down and gave his sermon. St Luke does not give us the content: there is the briefest reference, perhaps the closing words—'This text is being fulfilled today even as you listen' (St Luke 4.21). The eager anticipation, the enthralled attention as he spoke, turned from praise for his preaching ability to surprise that he should claim that Old Testament history was leading up to him. They were infuriated and intended to throw him to his death.

APPLICATION

Will you listen with confidence that this 'prophecy is being fulfilled today even as you listen'? 'The spirit of the Lord has been given to me, for he has anointed me.' (St Luke 4.18). There is no doubt in Luke's mind that Jesus is the anointed one: have you any doubt? In order to emphasise this truth Luke has placed this Galilean episode immediately after his account of the baptism and temptation of Jesus. This is to show that the Spirit of the Lord was on Jesus and that he had rejected any popular or quick ways to establish his kingship. 'He has sent me to bring good news to the poor' (St Luke 4.18). What does this mean? The good news of the gospel we can understand, but why 'to the poor'? The poor are the underprivileged, ignored so far as may conveniently be done by society. *They* are to be particularly selected? 'To the poor'—poor in spirit, those spiritually bereft or in despair; they need the good news. Whichever interpretation we give there is but one conclusion: the good news is for all men, for you 'today even as you listen', 'to proclaim liberty to captives' (St Luke 4.18). Last week we saw that imprisonment can be of more than one kind. 'To proclaim . . . to the blind new sight' (St Luke 4.18), this Jesus miraculously did. But blindness can be of more than physical blindness. Is our spiritual sight all that it might be? 'To set the downtrodden free' (St Luke 4.18). Do we see this as part of our Christian responsibility today? 'To proclaim the Lord's year of Favour' (St Luke 4.18). This was originally a prophecy that after the exile in Babylon, the Jewish people would be free once again to return to Jerusalem and to celebrate the Lord's year of favour. But, Jesus claimed that it was in fact fulfilled in him. How do we regard it? We do not have to wait until Christmas Day to proclaim it; 'this text is being fulfilled today even as you listen'. Each and every day we should pray and live with expectation.

SECOND SUNDAY BEFORE CHRISTMAS

Identification

St Matthew 11.15 (NEB) *'If you have ears, then hear.'*

INTRODUCTION

Deafness or partial hearing must be a tremendous disability. Imagine not being able to identify any sound. And yet identification may be defective even where the organ of hearing is perfect. 'If you have ears, then hear.'

Identification of the Promised One

John was imprisoned, but through others he heard what Jesus was doing. But, he was not altogether certain; and we may be a little puzzled that John was uncertain. Had he not known Jesus for years? We need to remember that John had been given the clue to the identity of Jesus only when our Lord came to the Jordan to be baptised by John; it was then that the sign was given, when the Holy Spirit descended as a dove upon Jesus. Obviously John had followed the career of Jesus with some care; but perhaps (like many of his contemporaries) his understanding of the true nature of Messiahship was defective and that is why he sent messengers to ask 'Are you the one who is to come, or are we to expect some other?' (St Matthew 11.3). The answer given to John was 'if you have ears, then hear' what I am doing; here is the definitive answer to your question: 'I am the Promised One.'

Identification of the forerunner

When John's disciples came to Jesus there were other people present, and it seems not unlikely that they heard the conversation. As we well know, many in Israel did not accept Jesus as the Messiah; nor did the disciples grasp the nature of Christ's Messiahship until after his Resurrection. But in this incident we find Jesus giving early indications that he is the Son of God—to John he had sent the message, 'hear what I have been doing'; to those who were with him after John's messengers depart he gave further evidence about himself, by identifying John the Baptist as the forerunner. 'Here is my herald, whom I send on ahead of you' (St Matthew 11.10). 'John is the destined Elijah, if you will but accept it' (St Matthew 11.14).

APPLICATION

Identical twins are difficult to identify; but the Mother finds no difficulty. When we apply for a passport we submit not only a photograph, we provide identification details about ourselves including any peculiar identification marks. When the police are investigating a crime they may hold an identification parade and almost certainly they will use the evidence of finger-prints. How do we identify a disciple of Jesus? He is first of all someone who accepts Jesus' claim that he is the Son of God; trusting the clues to our Lord's identity in the New Testament, he will identify the Babe of Bethlehem as the Word made Flesh. Secondly, he will identify himself with Christ being prepared to take up his cross; to be an agent of the kingdom. Thirdly, he heeds the call of the forerunner—repent, prepare the Way of the Lord. How will you be identified? Can Christ rely on your discipleship or must he look for another to do those things which you leave undone?

THE SUNDAY BEFORE CHRISTMAS

Order out of chaos

St Matthew 1.25 (NEB) '*And he named the child Jesus.*'

INTRODUCTION

It has been customary on Christmas morning to read the prologue to the Fourth Gospel where St John tells how 'Christ had existed with God the Father since the birth of time, and his 'coming' was really a 'becoming', the appearance of a pre-existent divine being at a certain moment and place in history'* ; whereas our popular Christmas services concentrate on the Lucan account of shepherds and the response of Mary 'My soul doth magnify the Lord'. St Matthew presents us with another opportunity of looking at the birth of Christ in relation to the Jewish expectation of a Messiah and through the response of Joseph to the critical and chaotic situation of Mary's pregnancy.

*A. Harvey, Companion to the New Testament (New English Bible) OUP & CUP 1970 p. 17.

St Matthew begins with the genesis of Jesus. In this he is concerned to establish the descent of Jesus from the Davidic line; but incidentally he shows how once more the Spirit of God brings order out of chaos for Joseph and Mary and through them and their experience for all mankind. Joseph was a man of principle; he was also a man of compassion who wished to spare Mary (if he could) from the scandalous consequences of her pre-marital pregnancy. Already betrothed to Joseph, Mary was committed to marrying him. The marriage contract had already been signed; all that remained was for the ceremony to be performed and for Mary to go and live in her husband's home. What could Joseph do? He could go on with the marriage; then the world would talk about their relationship before marriage. Not too much of a problem, but as it was not true that he was father of the child, what should he do, as a man of principle and as a just man? There were two alternatives open to him. He could bring his fiancee before a court of law and prove her guilty; but this he was not prepared to do. Alternatively, and it would seem that this is what he intended to do until there was divine intervention, he could repudiate the marriage contract before two witnesses and obtain a divorce. This would still leave the question of Mary's shame to be resolved by her family. But the Spirit of God intervened and brought order out of chaos for Joseph and Mary and for all mankind as a result.

On the eighth day after his birth, at his circumcision, Joseph named the child Jesus. In this way he adopted the child who became his son, bringing Jesus formally into his family and entitling him to be called 'a son of David'. 'And he named the child Jesus.' This was in obedience to the angelic vision, but this same Jesus is the one who brings order out of chaos for all mankind. In Hebrew the name 'Jesus' means 'God is salvation'; how appropriate a name for Our Lord who saves his people from their sins. In Genesis the Spirit of God brings cosmos out of chaos; in the *genesis* of Jesus the same spirit brings Christos over chaos bringing order out of rebellious society through his redemptive act.

We are asked to wait with expectation upon the celebration of the birth of the babe of Bethlehem; today's gospel stops short of the birth narrative. We are invited to share in the consternation of Joseph and Mary when confronted with the situation of the forthcoming birth. We are to remember their costly acceptance of the solution which was offered, and which they willingly embraced. We are to consider the relationship of principles and just behaviour alongside compassion and love in all our relationships. Above all we are to be mindful of the love of God.

THE SUNDAY AFTER CHRISTMAS

Make your mind up time

St Matthew 2.1 (JB). '*After Jesus had been born at Bethlehem in Judaea during the reign of King Herod, some wise men came to Jerusalem from the east.*'

INTRODUCTION

'Opportunity Knocks' retains its high place in the TV charts. This is perhaps due to its formula—the introduction of new faces and talents coupled with the show-biz possibility of the discovery of a new star. A star of celestial significance brought *magi* from the east to Jerusalem; and Matthew's exclusive reporting of this story suggests that perhaps he is saying, 'This is make your mind up time'. He brings several people to our notice and asks us to make a judgement—make *your* mind up about the infant king. To enable us to do this he presents us with two groups—THE TRADS and THE SEEKERS.

The trads (traditionalists)

These are represented by the Jews in the story. First there is Herod the King. Put yourself in his place receiving foreign visitors who announce that an infant king has been born; even

worse they insult your pride by referring to him as the infant
king of the *Jews* (so lacking in taste these gentiles!). As reigning
king in Jerusalem you know that no infant has been born to
you, and yet you have a nagging feeling because these visitors
seem well informed and so certain that this birth has taken
place. What can this mean? Can it be that the Messiah foretold
by the prophets has been born? He can't be much trouble as a
baby, though he might be the source of future trouble. Find out
whether there is any truth in what the magi claim. Best to play
along with them and ask them to let you know where they have
found him. Herod's eventual choice was an attempt to put the
infant king to death in the massacre of the innocents.

Secondly, among the trads, was the Sanhedrin whom Herod
called in for advice over where the Christ was to be born. When
another Herod was King it was the Sanhedrin who brought
Jesus to condemnation and crucifixion. Thirdly, the traditionalists were represented by 'the whole of Jerusalem', citizens said
to be perturbed by the news which the magi brought. Why
were they perturbed? Did they fear political factions and
allegiances? If he was the Messiah were their fears because they
were unready for his coming? The people of Jerusalem later
cried 'Crucify him'. What is certain is that the traditionalists
rejected him at birth and at his death.

The seekers

Flamboyant characters from the east with their caravan and
treasures, the magi were probably astrologers, certainly not
kings from the Orient. They were gentiles, who came seeking
to do homage, bringing their gifts, worthy of a king, of gold,
frankincense and myrrh. Detailed symbolic meanings have been
added. They were all gifts suitable for a king; they were also
the stock-in-trade of magicians. The seekers presented their
gifts and whichever way we interpret the occasions (as royal
presents suitable to majesty or the giving up of magical practices
by the magi) we must acknowledge that the magi have made
their minds up about the infant King of the Jews. In this they
may be deemed to be wise men.

'Opportunity knocks' for us each year as we are reminded of the visit of the magi; for us it is 'make your mind up time'. As regular churchgoers it is more likely that we are traditionalists; there is a warning here that the contemporary traditionalists of Jesus rejected him. Do we? Or do we cause others to reject him by our immovable conservatism? We would be wise to follow the example of the seekers—acknowledge our infant king, offer him our gifts and abandon all that hinders our loyal support as subjects of the King.

SECOND SUNDAY AFTER CHRISTMAS

Conscious Sonship

St Luke 2.42 (RSV) *'And when he was twelve years old, they went up according to custom.'*

INTRODUCTION

The gospels are silent about the early years of our Lord's life. Yet when Luke permits us a glimpse of the twelve-year-old in the temple at Jerusalem, we are able to discern already three aspects of his person.

Son of the law

'Think not that I have come to abolish the law and the prophets: I have come not to abolish them but to fulfil them' (St Matthew 5.17). This particular Passover pilgrimage was of great importance to Jesus. At the age of twelve Jesus, a Jewish boy, became *bar mitzvah*, a son of the Law, able to accept for himself the responsibilities and obligations to which Joseph and Mary had committed him at his circumcision. How well he had been prepared for that responsibility. Here he was, a country boy, brought up under the guidance of his parents and the local synagogue of Galilee, now able to discuss with leading scholars the interpretation of passages from the Old Testament. St Luke speaks of Jesus increasing in wisdom (St Luke 2.52) which in terms of Hebrew culture means understanding the ways of God as revealed in the law, the writings and the prophets. We see this wisdom exhibited throughout his ministry, here at the age of twelve it was evident in that competent teachers were happy to sit at his feet listening to him as he answered their questions and enquired of them.

Son of man

Jesus 'increased in favour with God and man' (St Luke 2.52). On this occasion in the temple he was in favour with the rabbis; a genius no doubt they thought him to be and longed to have him as their prize pupil. Enthralled and excited by this intellectual experience, Jesus exhibited typically youthful ignorance of the concern he was causing his parents by his absence from the caravan of Galilean pilgrims returning after the feast. He was so surprised that Joseph and Mary thought that he had treated them badly. Doubtless he would have liked to have remained at the temple; but as the son of man he returned home with them in obedience, living under parental control. There was no rejection of family ties, even though he had already some knowledge of his relationship to God the Father. Truly human!

Son of God

'Did you not know that I must be in my Father's house?' (St Luke 2.49). Mary and Joseph we are told did not understand this. Were they concerned that this was a wish to leave home and live in the city, even though expressed in a desire to be in the temple? Or were they puzzled by his use of the word 'Father'. Although God was spoken of as the Father of the Jewish people, the Old Testament does not display an understanding of a personal relationship between the individual and God. Jesus in his ministry emphasised this paternal relationship as a basis of our thinking about God and praying to him. Here at the age of twelve Jesus was already conscious of his unique relationship with God; he was his only Son.

15

All of us are sons of men with attendant responsibility to love our neighbours. All of us are sons of God by adoption and by grace; how deep is our relationship to God in prayer? Do we really think of God in this personal relationship or is the word 'Father' a customary one which unconsciously slips off our tongues in prayer. The scriptures both old and new, how well versed are we in these? Can we speak to the faith that is in us? Are we prepared to take trouble to learn some of the facts of our faith? Christian faith means using our intelligence. Jesus increased in wisdom, ought not we to make some attempt?

THIRD SUNDAY AFTER CHRISTMAS

Lamb of God

St John 1.29 (NEB) '*There is the lamb of God; it is he who takes away the sin of the world.*'

INTRODUCTION

Jesus was sacrified for us, the springtime of his ministry brought to an abrupt end '*the lamb of God . . . who takes away the sin of the world*'. This was foretold by the forerunner of Christ, John the Baptist. These words when spoken by John had a deeper impact on his disciples than they might have for us, owing to the cultural and religious traditions of the chosen people. (They do have an impact on us of course in their eucharistic use.) What of the original impact, long before the institution of the Lord's Supper?

The Substitute Sacrifice

John's disciples may have recalled the test of faith of their ancestor Abraham. Do you remember how this patriarch had long been denied the gift of an heir and then how in their old age he and Sarah were granted the birth of a son? In due time, acting in faith and by faith, Abraham took his only son Isaac and prepared to offer him as a sacrifice to Jehovah. But this was not to be; faith tested, faith attested. There was a moment of intervention, 'Do not harm the boy!' A lamb was caught in the thicket, a substitute sacrifice offered to the Lord.

The Lamb without blemish

Would they recall the institution of the Passover? According to this each householder (or with his nearest neighbour) was instructed to take a lamb without blemish to be slaughtered. The blood on the lintel to be a protecting sign; the flesh to be roasted and eaten quickly, none to be left over. 'Thou shall keep this day as a day of remembrance, and make it a pilgrim-feast, a festival to the Lord, you shall keep it generation after generation as a rule for all time' (Exodus 12.14). In a community so historically conditioned the paschal lamb retained an important place in the religious tradition of the people.

APPLICATION

The witness of John the Baptist 'There is the Lamb of God' brought Simon Peter and another to follow Jesus and to become his disciples. Some three years later they were to learn the significance of the saying that Jesus was (and is) the Paschal Lamb 'who takes away the sin of the world' through the substitute sacrifice of Calvary—substitute, that is, for sinners. Just before the sacrifice on the cross the disciples were given a new meaning to the Passover at the Lord's Supper: 'Do this in remembrance of me.' We, like them, share in the Christian Passover. We are protected by the Blood of Christ. We are fed by the sacramental Body of Christ, if, like Abraham, we receive him by faith: Jesus, the innocent lamb that was slain for us and all mankind. We cannot open a newspaper without reading of innocent suffering in the world: children in Vietnam, civilians in Northern Ireland, and innocent victims of our carelessness on the roads. All are consequences of human sin. What would Jesus have us do about the innocent lambs that are slain today?

FOURTH SUNDAY AFTER CHRISTMAS

Discipleship

St John 1.39 (NEB) *'Come and see.'*

INTRODUCTION

Discipline! What are your reactions to this word? Does it immediately conjure up military discipline, parental control or school authority? Discipline can also be applied to an area of study and in this relationship it is akin to discipleship. Universities began with disciples learning from masters. Plato and Socrates had their disciples; so had John the Baptist and Jesus. In today's gospel we heard how discipleship began for some of the apostles, and from this account we can learn something of the nature of Christian discipleship for us.

APPLICATION

Taking the first step

Two men, one of them identified as Andrew, had already been attracted to the teaching of John the Baptist as they sought a deeper meaning for life. From the chance remark of the Baptist 'Look there is the lamb of God' these men followed after Jesus. *They* had taken the first step; though with an inadequate appreciation of their future discipleship. Initially they thought of Jesus as a teacher and assumed he had the equivalent of a small school. However imperfect our understanding of discipleship it is necessary that we should take the first step. *'I turn to Christ'* is a preliminary to our experiencing Christ's offering of himself to us; 'Come and see'. Our discipleship must be characterised by expectation.

Spreading the news

Andrew and the other disciple followed Jesus, because of what John the Baptist had said about him, 'We have found the Messiah' (St John 1.41). Nathaniel is brought to Jesus by what Philip told him. Some say religion is caught not taught; and there is some truth in this saying. But this does not excuse us from talking about Jesus; spreading the good news of the gospel. There are many who owe their commitment to Christ through what they heard at their mother's knee or from a devout Sunday School teacher. Think of those who have influenced you. See to it that you influence others.

Being missionaries

We do not read much about Andrew in the gospels; we read much more about his brother Simon Peter. Yet Andrew was the first missionary; it was he who brought his brother to Jesus. Who did the greater service?

There is something romantic about being an overseas missionary. But here, where we are, is a missionary opportunity. William Temple, commenting on this verse had this to say: 'We never know who is doing the greatest work for God. Here is a man who holds great office in the Church and preaches to multitudes; yet at the end, all he has done is to keep things from falling back. And there is a girl, poor and uneducated, of whom no one ever thinks; but because she is loving and devout she sows the seed of life in a child entrusted to her care who grows up to be a missionary pioneer, or Christian statesman, or profound theologian—shaping the history of nations or the thought of generations. Andrew findeth his own brother; perhaps it is as great a service to the Church as ever any man did.'* Who have we brought to Christ? To whom have we said, 'Come and see?'

*William Temple, *Readings in St John's Gospel* (St Martin's Library edition) 1963 p. 28.

FIFTH SUNDAY AFTER CHRISTMAS

Temples of God

St John 2.21 (NEB) *'But the temple he was speaking of was his body.'*

We can well understand the attitude which Jesus adopted towards the traders and money-changers in the Temple. Let us spend some time considering the indignation of the Temple authorities and the grounds for their anger as they questioned his authority to act in such a way. The Temple was not that built by Solomon; it was the Temple begun in the reign of Herod the Great about forty-six years before the time of this particular incident. The Temple authorities were not unnaturally proud of their achievement in the rebuilding of the Temple to the glory of Jehovah. Doubtless they could justify their economic and financial policy on the grounds that the rebuilding was not yet complete and additional capital was required to complete the project; in addition to the running costs. They were blinded by their concern for the building and the suggestion that this new Temple would be destroyed was sacrilegious. Add to this the absurd claim that it could be rebuilt in three days and we can understand their indignation. Their involvement with the ecclesiastical building blinded them from recognising the messianic significance of Jesus saying: 'In three days I will raise it again' (St John 2.19). St John suggests that it was only after the resurrection of Jesus that his disciples recalled this incident and understood the implications of his claim.

APPLICATION

'But the temple he was speaking of was his body.' We are now the Body of Christ and all temples of the Holy Spirit. What can we learn from this incident that may help us to be more effective temples of the living God? Our lives should be ordered by a recurrent recognition and acknowledgement that they are to be appropriate dwelling-places for God. Like the Temple authorities in Jerusalem we may have got our priorities wrong, both individually and corporately. Are we cluttered up with worldly ambitions dominated by the profiteering of the market-place or stock-market? As churchmen are we over anxious about buildings, keeping our own show going though others advise amalgamation of parishes or ecumenical experiment? The Temple situation in Jerusalem led to exploitation of the people who were coming to fulfil their religious obligations. Temple dues could not be paid in the currency of the market-place and the currency exchange was to the advantage of the Temple money-changers. As temples of the Holy Spirit how do we deal with other people? Do we exploit our employees? Are we fair to our employers? Is our daily life in accord with our Christian profession? Or can the outward appearance of my temple of God show a false façade which hides the inner reality which cannot be hidden from God? Jesus had a zeal for his Father's house, a zeal exhibited when he came to the Temple as a twelve-year-old and now again as he cleared out the traders and the money-changers. How do we stand as temples of God?

SIXTH SUNDAY AFTER CHRISTMAS

Living water

> St John 4.14 (NEB) '*The water that I shall give him will be an inner spring always welling up for eternal life.*'

INTRODUCTION

From the vantage point of the hillside the sprawling streets of the city can be seen climbing the several hills from the valley of the Don which lies at the heart of the city. On a summer's day, when the sun pierces the smoke haze, the landscape can be more clearly distinguished. In the near distance the Wednesday football ground lies empty and silent; on the hill to the right can be seen the growing campus of the university. The smoke haze (now considerably lessened by more recent legislation) is a constant reminder that the health, wealth, livelihood and fame of Sheffield are all dependent upon steel. The hillside of this vantage point lies at the beginning of the Pennine range, which separates the counties of the rival roses; making certain that Sheffield lies within allegiance to the White Rose. A rural scene enveloped by the sprawl of an expanding city.

At the foot of the hill, huddled together as though for protection from the prevailing winds, lies a row of cottages, their stones blackened by the soot of many years close to industry. It is the absence of an amenity which brings this reminiscence to mind. There were no taps of running water. Instead the occupants had to walk some three hundred or more yards to where a running stream of cool, clear water emptied itself into a stone trough which served as a well. In the severest of winters the constant running of water meant that it never froze; in the driest of spells it may be reduced to a trickle, but to my knowledge never did it cease. After racing around the hills as boys we knew this water to be very refreshing: it tasted so cool and so different from that which came out of the tap at home about half a mile away. We could only cup our hands to get a supply; but the cottagers brought their buckets when they came to that living water to supply their needs of drink, washing, cooking and laundry.

APPLICATION

'Sir,' the Samaritan woman said to Jesus, 'you have no bucket and the well is deep. How can you give me "living water"?' Jesus promised that each and everyone of us can receive that inner spring of 'living water'. A spring that never fails to satisfy. Indeed it is always welling up; a constant renewal of the spring of eternal life. Christ who, on the cross of Calvary, cried 'I thirst', promises that we shall never thirst any more, if only we thirst after Jesus, who is the living water of eternal life. This very morning we experience that presence and renewal within us at this eucharist.

SEVENTH SUNDAY AFTER CHRISTMAS

Workers for the Kingdom

St Matthew 20.7 (NEB) *'Go and join the others in the vineyard.'*

INTRODUCTION

The parable we have just had read presents us with three problems in our understanding of its meaning. The employment requirements of the vine harvesting are different from anything we encounter in our own experience. The time-scale of one working day also presents a problem of interpretation. But our interpretation is further complicated by St Matthew's presentation of the parable as a 'Kingdom of Heaven' saying of Jesus. Many commentators doubt if this was its original setting and suggest that Jesus probably told the story when his association with tax collectors and sinners had brought him into conflict with the Pharisees. But are the difficulties of interpretation as great as all that?

Kingdom of Heaven

The Kingdom of Heaven has been inaugurated in Christ himself; though the fullness of its reality awaits a final consummation in God's good time. In the meantime, all Christians are agents or servants of the Kingdom and the relationship to the King does not depend upon when we were born or who we are. There are no priority places (St Matthew brings this out in his next chapter when the sons of Zebedee seek places of distinction); nor can we earn our way to Heaven. The twentieth-century Christian has the same relationship to Christ as the first century Christian; it is a relationship of faith and service.

Opportunity for service

The time-scale of the parable is one working day; when the main aim of the operation was to ensure that the grapes were harvested to the full. The objection raised of equal payment seems to be in accord with sound economic reasoning, and we can imagine the reaction of trade unions today to such a situation. The important issue for a servant of the Kingdom is, however, whether or not he is prepared to give himself to the full in circumstances and places where he is called to serve. We are not to be concerned about the call of others in the service of Christ, it is Christ's call that 'some are to be apostles, some prophets, some evangelists, some pastors and teachers'. We are called to get on with our own work 'to the building up of the body of Christ' (Ephesians 4.11). Some may be called to serve for a 'short' time; others for a 'longer' time.

Equality of opportunity

We are called to be workers for the Kingdom, in that long succession from the first disciples. The area of work may differ; but we all have an equal opportunity to share with Christians of all ages in that benefit which Christ obtained for all who have faith in him and are willing to be the servant Body of Christ in their particular area of harvesting.

EIGHTH SUNDAY AFTER CHRISTMAS

Continuous worship

St John 4.24 (NEB) '*God is spirit, and those who worship him must worship in spirit and in truth.*'

INTRODUCTION

Historical evidence and contemporary practice both suggest that man has tended to localise the object of his worship. Primitive man located 'gods' in the natural phenomenon and made them the object of his worship. Twentieth-century technical man may well localise his object of worship in a pop star or sports personality or even some object of his possessions, such as his car.

We are reminded in today's gospel that the Jews and the

Samaritans had located the worship of God (and the presence of God) in the Temple or on the mountain. Indeed this identification of the true place of worship was a major cause of division between the Samaritans and the Jews. It has often proved convenient for man to localise the object of his worship; and 'localising' the worship of God is no exception. If the true place of worshipping Jehovah was the Temple in Jerusalem, it proved convenient to worship only when in Jerusalem at the great feasts (not unlike our festival worshippers at Christmas and Easter) and perhaps to be unmindful of God's presence during the rest of the year—the absent God!

The Church has not altogether escaped this problem and with it another danger appears. We can tend to make God into an idol, limiting him to some noble conception which does not sufficiently measure up to the truth that 'God is spirit'. Whereas an excess of the medieval church was to localise God in the Mass (in the elevation of the host); it proved also a Reformation excess to localise God in the sacred scriptures.

APPLICATION

If it proves convenient to our limited understanding of God to localise his presence in some way or other, the question arises—How can we avoid the dangers which arise from such a limited vision? Jesus provides us with the answer—'God is spirit', which Archbishop Temple says 'is active energy, alive and purposive, but free from the temporal and spatial limitations of matter'.* In other words God is dynamic. In the context of the eucharist the Bread symbolises this: God's creative provision and man's activity. 'Those who worship him must worship him in spirit and in truth.' Our worship should never cease, our daily round of activity should be a worthwhile offering to the Lord, our continuous worship; thus we avoid the danger of localising worship in our liturgical worship in Church on Sundays. But there is a danger the other way: not to worship in Church on Sundays, with our concentration on the divine, could mean that

*William Temple, *Readings in St John's Gospel* (St Martin's Library edition) 1963 p. 63.

worship could go out of our lives completely. Continuous worship must be our aim. We need to balance the localisation of Sunday worship by worthwhile living day by day; the eucharist helps us to explore the essence of worship to the full.

NINTH SUNDAY BEFORE EASTER

Spreading the secrets

St Luke 8.10 (NEB) *'It has been granted to you to know the secrets of the kingdom of God.'*

INTRODUCTION

Can you keep a secret? Only perhaps with great difficulty. The secrets of the kingdom of God are not intended to be kept as our secrets; we are all required to make them known. Jesus told the disciples that they were fortunate to be able to discover the true meaning of God's purposes, although it is not altogether clear that they understood the secrets of the kingdom until they possessed the understanding of Christ's victorious death and passion. He had to explain to them on this occasion the meaning of the parable, but in so doing he enabled them and us to discover hidden truths. Fortunate to possess the secrets of the kingdom, we have the associated responsibility of making them known. How? In the parable of the sower and the seeds Christ the teacher shows us the way; an approach identical with much contemporary educational method.

APPLICATION

(1) *Man-motivated*

There is a temptation to say that Jesus' teaching was man-centred as he frequently illustrates the secrets of the kingdom from human situations. His aim is God-directed; the means by which he seeks to direct is through the medium of human experience and endeavour. Modern educational methods emphasise child-centred rather than subject-centred teaching.

In our spreading of the secrets of the kingdom of God perhaps the right approach is *man-motivated;* this means starting with a person where he is, his capacity of understanding, the way his mind works. Like Jesus, our aim must be God-directed, but the means *man-motivated.* Did not God choose to reveal himself most fully in the Word made flesh? Jesus began the disclosure of the secrets of the kingdom through human experience; the sower and the seeds.

(2) *Discovery learning*
'All truth is clear, self-evident and compelling to those who have seen the point' (i) How many times has this been your experience that in a group, some immediately grasp the point, others require further explanation to get the point. A joke which has to be explained is a failure; but the secrets of the kingdom are no joke. A parable is a means of discovery learning.

> 'Jesus's secret—his new conception of the meaning of the king-dom—was open for everyone to see and hear, but even an open secret remains a secret from those who do not wish to learn it. Jesus told parables partly to accommodate profound truth to simple minds, partly to elicit from his hearers a decision about the story which would at the same time be a decision about their own lives, partly to distinguish the perceptive, who were open to receive the secrets of the kingdom, from the dull of under-standing, to whom the parables were stories and nothing more.'

(ii) In passing on the secrets of the kingdom we must allow people to discover for themselves. Theologians are constantly engaged in discovery learning. Are we?

(3) *Related to living*
In the parable of the sower (and on other occasions) Jesus used living situations as the means of disclosing the secrets of the kingdom. Educationists may disagree on the contents of a syllabus or whether secondary education should be compre-hensive; but each would be enthused by the prime aim that education is for living. But what can fit people for living more

effectively than the Christian way? There is no doubt that many are searching for the meaning of life today. They cannot see the hidden secret of the life of the church lived out in Christian spirituality. It remains our task to show them that the secrets of the kingdom are related to living.

EIGHTH SUNDAY BEFORE EASTER

Making men whole

St Mark 1.40 (NEB) *'Once he was approached by a leper, who knelt before him begging his help.'*

INTRODUCTION

Modern drugs have enabled doctors to cure leprosy. Even so to see a leper today, as one still can in many parts of the under-developed world, is to know at once why it was that the disease was so dreaded in the time of Jesus. But when Jesus healed 'a leper who knelt before him begging his help' he made him whole. It meant that he was able to return to society (that is why he had to go to the priest to get the certificate of clearance), he could return to his family and above all he could become truly himself.

APPLICATION

There are many ills in our contemporary world; some of which can be cured by specialist help of all engaged in medicine. There are many ills which are social and require the attention of politicians and specialists in social welfare. Yet all this pro-fessional range of help does not meet the total need of making men whole. It still needs the healing power of Christ and that power is ours as the Body of Christ. This does not mean that we can set ourselves up in opposition to the skills of medicine; indeed we should be acting contrary to Christ if we ignored the benefits of the skills granted to men by God.

(1) Restored to society

There are many men and women who are alienated from society. This may be of their own making—the dropouts, the drug addicts, the tramps. Others may have been alienated by the attitude of society towards them—race, educational limitations and class. Sometimes the estrangement is loneliness following upon bereavement, loneliness through inability in old age, loneliness through fear—how many people in our large cities sit in at night behind locked doors and barred windows living in fear of the intruder. And strangely enough there is the lonely person who attends our churches; he may be active in some of our organisations, perhaps on the PCC. This is the range of possibilities to which we have to act in Christ's name in making men whole.

(2) Restored to family

The leper in our gospel today remains anonymous; but there is the possibility that he returned to his home whether as a son or as a husband and father. The two words—broken family—are sufficient to remind us of this sickness in our contemporary world; people who once loved one another, or thought they did, and are now separated. The generation gap: how are we dealing with this in our own family? How do we exercise Christian parental control? How do we respond to parental concern? A whole world here of sickness to be dealt with.

(3) Becoming truly human

Looking back in history it is easy for us to recognise the inhumanity of the industrial revolution. Are we so easily aware of the inhumanity of our present technological society? Unemployment, redundancy, bankruptcy, mobility of labour; these are phrases and words until experienced within our own small world. But they are realities of today and as Christians we cannot ignore giving a helping hand. The leper in the gospel story knew his need; he was also certain of what Jesus could do for him. The problem with many of us is that we do not know what we need to become fully human. The symptoms may not be easily discerned; but there is an underlying cause, the sickness of the soul. This needs the cure which only Christ can bring through the agency of his church. It can first be experienced through the love shown by any Christian towards another. It can be enlightened by the knowledge of Christ; preaching of his Word is not limited to the pulpit nor to the priest. It may need the sacramental gifts which Christ gave to his Church and priesthood. 'If only you will, you can cleanse me.' 'Indeed I will; be clean again.'

SEVENTH SUNDAY BEFORE EASTER

Stilling the storm
St Mark 4.39 (NEB) '*Hush! Be still!*'

INTRODUCTION

How do you interpret the stilling of the storm? Do you see on the one hand: Jesus so fatigued and tired that he sleeps unaware of the raging storm, or is this evidence of his supreme trust in God? Do you see on the other hand: the 'fishermen' disciples (who ought to be experienced in storm conditions) now incompetent and ill-prepared, and frightened and lacking in faith? Perhaps the understanding of the primitive church can bring us to a deeper appreciation of the stilling of the storm.

We have to place ourselves in the position of 'hearers', remembering the oral tradition of Christianity before the gospels were written down. Imagine an eager group of Christian converts listening to stories of what Jesus had said or done. This would be a favourite story and doubtless would be interpreted against the background of the Jewish scriptures. The written account reflects the moulding of the story in successive retelling, where there is no doubt that the early Christians found in it practical encouragement as they faced the storms of life. What were these insights? How helpful can they be to us?

Often when we have cares and worries we are unable to sleep at night. Restless, we toss and turn in bed, like a storm-swept sea. The ability of Jesus to sleep would be seen by the early Christians as evidence of his perfect trust in the sustaining and protective power of God. It is due to the imperfection of our faith in God that we are not always able to set aside fears and worries. We need the faith of Jesus and of the psalmist, 'Now I will lie down in peace, and sleep; for thou alone, O Lord, makest me live unafraid' (Psalm 4.8). Why did Jesus have this trust in God? Steeped in the Hebrew myths of creation he would have learned how that God in the act of creation, according to one tradition, had been involved in a desperate and victorious battle with the forces of chaos and evil. The storm was a metaphor often used to indicate the evil forces in the world. Christ's stilling of the waves would be seen as a characteristically divine act. 'Who can this be? Even the winds and waves obey him' (St Mark 4.41). There are many times in the history of Israel that it appeared to them that God had absented himself. Perhaps he is asleep—'Awake, why sleepest thou, O Lord?' (Psalm 44.23). Jesus was not indifferent to their plight on the storm-swept sea. Jesus would not be indifferent to the storms of life of the early Christians and this gave them encouragement as they faced suffering and persecution. Jesus is not indifferent to the storms of our lives, where the merest troublesome patch seems to be overwhelming, even though our prayer is not accompanied by perfect faith. The prayer of the fishermen, 'Master, we are sinking. Do you not care?' did not go unheeded even though their faith was weak. In all the storm of our lives Jesus says, 'Hush! Be still'. Amidst the rush of contemporary living we need to be still and to know God.

SIXTH SUNDAY BEFORE EASTER
(Lent 1)

Power

St Luke 4.6 (JB) *'I will give you all this power.'*

INTRODUCTION

We live in a technological age where the technologist manipulates resources to meet men's needs. In this he exercises power. Power always involves manipulation whether of men or things. The exercise of power needs to be God-directed, if it is not to be used wrongly.

Manipulating resources

If Jesus had turned the stones into bread this would have represented the exercise of power over natural resources; in this case making a part of creation act contrary to its nature. If Jesus had used power in this way it would have been to satisfy a personal need, but Jesus was not prepared to manipulate creation merely to satisfy his hunger.

Manipulating men

This is particularly evident in politics. Today we can see this exercised in several ways. We cannot claim that the Westminster democratic system is free from manipulation. In earlier centuries political power was exercised by kings and this is why the devil promised Jesus political control of the kingdoms visible from the mountain-top. Easy acquisition of a kingdom! Manipulation of men can be exercised in other ways; in what we teach them or how they are organised for effective bargaining in industry.

Manipulating the will

Pop-stars and soccer idols exercise an influence often unrelated to their particular skills. The soccer star found guilty of drug offences; the pop-star whose sex-life displays a disregard for the conventions of society. In the exercise of their liberty they are manipulating the will of others; it matters not whether this is a deliberate attempt. The devil wanted Jesus to make a spectacular display which would have hit the headlines—JUMP FROM THE TEMPLE. Jesus was not prepared to attract followers with such a show-biz spectacular.

APPLICATION

All of us are aware of power exercised by others. We grumble when government measures adversely affect our circumstances. We lose sympathy with striking miners when their action results in the loss of light and heat in our homes. But do we recognise the power each one of us exercises? How do you manipulate resources? Should a typist use her employer's time and equipment to type personal letters during office hours? How do we manipulate our family? Paul Tournier suggests that all families operate a parliamentary-spirit, each member judging and manipulating the situation to achieve his own ends. How do we manipulate the will of others? The boy who persuades a girl to engage in pre-marital intercourse contrary to her wishes. The girl or boy who introduces another to smoking. God has given power to each one of us. How shall we use that power? We have before us the example of Jesus when he was tempted in the wilderness.

FIFTH SUNDAY BEFORE EASTER
EASTER
(Lent 2)

We are the Kingdom

St Matthew 12.28 (NEB) '*Then be sure that the kingdom of God has already come upon you.*'

INTRODUCTION

Millions of words have been written by theologians on 'The kingdom of God'. In thirteen words Jesus, in the gospel for today, proclaims 'then be sure that the kingdom of God has already come upon you'. Addressed to the Pharisees, who were questioning the source of his healing powers, these words are pertinent today. One interpretation of the kingdom of God is that it is within each individual Christian and it follows that through us God is seeking to establish his kingdom; and for that we daily pray, live and work.

Today's gospel also indicates that the kingdom is not established and maintained without conflict. This conflict is being fought on the universal stage of human history. It is also being waged in each human life. This reflects the division that is in man. Endowed with the Spirit, the distinguishing mark of man in creation, 'it is true also that spirit itself can become perverted so that we can speak of 'evil spirit' and 'spiritual evil'.* Division is of the devil and a consequence of rebellion against the Spirit of God. Jesus speaks of a divided kingdom, a divided city and a divided household; all signs of the end and destruction.

Although there is a conflict in our human striving it is through the Spirit of God that we have access to the Father. (Ephesians 2.18). It is by our adoption as sons that we can cry, 'Abba Father' (Romans 8.15). It is by the Spirit of God that Jesus drove out devils (St Matthew 12.28). It is by the same Spirit that we are enabled to play our role in establishing the kingdom of God. How responsive are we to the role which we have to play?

APPLICATION

Jesus warned us of the dangers of division. Today the Spirit is forcing Christians to recognise the dangers of the divided church. Ecumenical dialogue and endeavour is a feature of current ecclesiastical concern. Yet, when the Church of England was provided with its first practical exercise in church unity with the Methodist Church there arose doubts and divisions. Supporters of the scheme urged that the realities of the situation proved beyond doubt that this was the only way forward. The opposers were equally convinced that the scheme was divisive and therefore ought not to be implemented on any count.

*John Macquarie: *Paths in Spirituality* S.C.M. 1972 p. 43.

Conflict among Christians; all of whom pray for the guidance of the Holy Spirit. What then are we looking for when we seek to distinguish the workings of the Spirit? It is quite certain that the Spirit cannot be and will not be restricted by the human endeavours to determine the pattern of God's purposes. Firstly, the Spirit is elusive. 'The wind blows where it wills; you hear the sound of it, but you do not know where it comes from, or where it is going' (John 3.8). Secondly, the Spirit of God is dynamic and we find that our lives and outlooks are too restrictive and we are too set in our ways. Our prejudices, nay even our principles, will need to be broken if the elusive and dynamic Spirit of God is to work effectively through us as agents of the King.

FOURTH SUNDAY BEFORE EASTER
(Lent 3)

Vows of significance

St Luke 9.23 (NEB). *'And to all he said, "If anyone wishes to be a follower of mine, he must leave self behind; day after day he must take up his cross, and come with me".'*

INTRODUCTION

A nun occupied the pulpit of a parish church during a Lenten course on 'Servants of the Church'. Her assigned brief was to show how nuns and monks serve the church and God. She chose to speak about 'the quality of the religious life', what they seek to be rather than what they aim to do. This quality depended upon growth in community aided by the traditional vows of poverty, chastity and obedience. A quality of living demonstrating to all Christians the need to aim at a similar life of quality under different daily circumstances.

In the course of her sermon she said, 'You are *the* religious community here in this parish'. Each congregation *is* the local religious community and we are admitted to it by vows of significance. At baptism we may be thought to be entering our Christian novitiate; at confirmation to be taking our individual life vows. How can the traditional vows and way of life of a Religious be a guide to the quality of Christian living in the world?

APPLICATION

The vows made at baptism and confirmation are identical. At baptism (as infants) we are offered to the Lord. At confirmation we make a life-long commitment.

(1) *Poverty: 'I turn to Christ'*

The monastic vow of giving up personal possessions is not a negative act; nor does it mean that the community does not have any economic problems or possess material things. The prime purpose is to cultivate a complete dependence upon God. *'I turn to Christ'* implies the same condition of utter dependence and a recognition that our needs are met by God in his creative provision. This necessary quality of Christian living needs to be evident in the materialistic world in which we live.

(2) *Chastity: 'I repent of my sins'*

The nun was careful to point out that celibacy is not a superior state. It is one way, to which some are called, to express a true self-giving love for God. An adequate love for God is always prevented by our sinfulness, so that the repenting of our sins is essential to our desire to love God. Repent means to turn around, to leave self behind; which Jesus said is necessary to Christian discipleship. The chastity of the religious also serves as a reminder of how Christians ought to use the sexual instincts implanted in us all. True love is self-giving, not self-imposing; another quality of Christian living which needs to be demonstrated in this permissive age.

(3) *Obedience: 'I renounce evil'*

No one entering a monastery or a convent to test a vocation to the Religious life enters a community already perfect. Nor does living a community life mean that the circumstances for Christian obedience are any easier; indeed they may be more difficult. Obedience to the Will of God requires that we renounce evil for all evil is contrary to God's Will. Our renunciation of evil at baptism and confirmation binds us in obedience to God. Our failure to completely obey means that time and time again we need to renounce evil, to repent and to seek forgiveness.

(4) Daily performance

Of any disciple Jesus said, 'day after day he must take up his cross'. Vows taken by a Religious, baptismal and confirmation vows taken by all of us are all vows of significance requiring daily performance. Vows are hard to keep and it is only through God's sustaining grace that we are enabled to grow in our Christian commitment. Are we prepared for this daily struggle? Will we respond to Christ's invitation 'Come with me'? It will be the Way of the Cross.

THIRD SUNDAY BEFORE EASTER
(Lent 4)

Christ's glory revealed

St Luke 9.32 (NEB) *'When they awoke, they saw his glory.'*

INTRODUCTION

The disciples had found it difficult to accept that Christ's glory was to be fulfilled through his death. A moment of high spiritual intensity had been experienced when Peter had claimed that Jesus was 'God's Messiah' (St Luke 9.21); only to be shattered when Jesus told them that the way ahead was rejection, punishment, pain and death. They were so surprised that the Messiah should come to such an end that they little heeded that he also said that he would 'be raised again on the third day'

(St Luke 9.22). The intense experience on a spiritual peak had been followed by a plateau of uncertainty and doubt. It was then that Jesus provided Peter, James and John with a momentary glimpse of his glory on the Mount of Transfiguration.

APPLICATION

From time to time we all experience spiritual heights when we are particularly aware that we are in the presence of God. There are also many times when we cannot feel that presence; perhaps it is because our eyes are heavy and we are in a deep sleep. When we awake then again the glory of Christ is revealed. Perhaps only a glimpse of that glory; yet enough to encourage us towards the heavenly vision of the glory that shall be revealed hereafter. Such a glimpse Peter, James and John had on the Mount of Transfiguration. For a time they kept this experience to themselves. For a time we may keep a personal experience of Christ to ourselves, but then like Peter, James and John we must speak out concerning the glory of Christ. When the disciples revealed details of that particular revelation of Christ's glory they provided us with four facets which may help us to experience and declare the glory of Jesus.

(1) *His Sonship*

The glory of God had been experienced over the centuries. Moses had stood in the presence of God before the burning bush. God had revealed to Peter that Jesus was 'God's Messiah' (St Luke 9.21). Again there is confirmation of Peter's faith 'This is my Son, my chosen' (St Luke 9. 36).

(2) *His destiny*

Moses and Elijah 'spoke of his departure, the destiny he was to fulfil in Jerusalem' (St Luke 9.31). This is confirmed that the way ahead was the way of the cross. We are to seek the glory of Christ shining victorious on Calvary.

(3) *His purpose*

Moses and Elijah represent not just the Law and the Prophets, they were representative of the old order based on the old covenant. Jesus enacted the new covenant inaugurated on Calvary.

(4) *His eternal glory*

In Jesus past, present and future are all brought together. He is the fulfilment of the law and the prophets; indeed 'no single thing was created without him' (St John 1.3). The present (in relation to the Transfiguration) was the Way of the Cross, the Resurrection and the Ascension. The future, in God's chosen time, a return in glory. Our way is the way of the Cross; granted from time to time a glimpse of his glory. An encouragement as our lives are transfigured (transformed) into his likeness by the Spirit of God.

SECOND SUNDAY BEFORE EASTER
(Passion Sunday)

Servants and slaves

St Mark 10.32 (JB) '*They were on the road, going up to Jerusalem; Jesus was walking on ahead of them; they were in a daze, and those who followed were apprehensive.*'

INTRODUCTION

Many pilgrims will be making for the Holy Land this Eastertide; there to follow the Way of the Cross. Every year the church invites us on a similar pilgrimage in thought and prayer. For most Christians this pilgrimage begins next Sunday when we remember Christ's entry into Jerusalem. But to the discerning we have already entered on to that annual pilgrimage today, Passion Sunday, as we heard in the gospel, 'They were on the road, going up to Jerusalem' (St Mark 10.32). Following the pattern of the eastern shepherd (and he is our shepherd) Jesus was leading the procession. It is not at all clear how many were with him as he led the way to Jerusalem; certainly there were more than the twelve for he took them aside on the journey to tell them for the third time of his passion and its sequel.

They were in a daze

Was this because Jesus was confidently striding before them with his face set towards Jerusalem? Jerusalem had been the real centre of hostility towards him throughout his ministry. The kind of mob he led was hardly equipped to take the city by storm; it is doubtful whether they could even defend themselves against the occupying forces of Rome. Perhaps they were in a daze for as yet they did not understand what Jesus had told them about his kingdom and his rule. A third time he had to tell them of the passion ahead and Mark perhaps includes the account of John and James' request at this point in his gospel to underline the misunderstanding of the disciples. If they still expected that Jesus would walk into Jerusalem and overthrow the Roman domination they could equally be in a daze when they considered the force and equipment at his disposal.

They were apprehensive

They had cause to be. There was mounting opposition to Jesus from those in authority. They could be in no doubt that Jesus was taking a terrible risk by going up to Jerusalem in view of this mounting powerful opposition. And what of their reception, what would happen to them?

They were very human

James and John seeking positions of importance, and the others indignant when they heard.

APPLICATION

On our way to the heavenly Jerusalem where Jesus has gone ahead there are times when we are not unlike the followers on the road to Jerusalem with Jesus. We find ourselves in a daze; it may be when we have suffered a bereavement and we are not at all certain of God's sustaining love. Our grief may be so great that we are numbed and unaware of Jesus' presence. We are apprehensive and our faith may even waver. We are very human, even within the Church, where we have differences of opinion and stand by our prejudices and principles. It is then that we have to be reminded by Jesus that 'anyone who wants to become great among you must be your servant, and anyone who wants to be first among you must be slave to all' (St Mark 10.43, 44). Are you prepared to be a servant (with all that this involves) or slave (with no rights whatsoever) for Christ?

SUNDAY BEFORE EASTER
(Palm Sunday)

Directive fulfilled

St Matthew 21.6 (JB) 'So the disciples went out, and did as Jesus had told them.'

INTRODUCTION

How would Jesus enter Jerusalem? He himself made the choice. But the execution of that decision was dependent upon the co-operation of two disciples who 'went out and did as Jesus had told them'. Later reflection prompted Matthew to see in the triumphal entry the fulfilment of prophecy. On that first Palm Sunday it would be doubtful whether the disciples were conscious of this prophetic fulfilment. They had a more specific and immediate task to perform. They reacted to what Jesus told them to do by doing it. His instructions were sufficient. Yet the fulfilment of these instructions was a necessary prelude to the triumphal entry into Jerusalem.

They went

This is perhaps the most extraordinary thing about the Palm Sunday story. They were to go to a nearby village where they would find tethered a donkey with her colt. Villagers were readily aware of the presence of strangers and they would be particularly on the alert as many pilgrims would be passing through on their way to keep the Passover. Not all who passed through the village would be pilgrims; there may be un-desirables ready to cause trouble. We have a parallel today when rowdy and destructive elements often turn a peaceful protest into a conflict with authority. One way or another the villagers of Bethphage would be on their guard and as soon as the disciples began to untether the animals they would be challenged. They were prepared to fulfil the directive with the only *title* they could give—'The Master needs them and will send them back directly' (St Matthew 21.5). Nevertheless, they went on this extraordinary errand; they relied on Jesus' directions.

They found

On arriving at the village they found all just as Jesus had told them. Matthew does not tell us whether they were challenged. The account in Mark's gospel (which differs in some detail) tells us that they were challenged by some men; not surprisingly as they found the donkey 'near a door in the open street' (St Mark 11.4). The men, however, seemed to have been satisfied with the answer that the disciples gave.

They brought

The mission was fulfilled by bringing the chosen beast to Jesus. This brought immediate reactions from the disciples and the crowd. The disciples determined that Jesus should have as comfortable a ride as possible and improvised a saddle with their coats. The crowd, who were glad to see Jesus, spread branches from the trees and sang triumphant Hosannas.

They entered

This motley crowd entered Jerusalem. It is not an exaggeration to suggest a parallel entry of guitar-singing hippies into the market-place of any ancient and respectable market town in England today. The entry turned 'the whole city . . . in turmoil' (St Matthew 21.10).The main point is that it made people ask, 'Who is this?' (St Matthew 21.11).

The road from Bethphage to Jerusalem has now been extended to every part of the world as the gospel has been preached to successive generations. This week we are sent by Jesus to follow in his footsteps as he travelled to the inevitable conflict and his death on the cross, so that we can share more wonderfully in the truth of his resurrection on Easter Day. It is the Way of the Cross; we have our guide, the Holy Spirit. We have to show in our lives our commitment to Christ so that others ask, 'Who is this Jesus who makes life so much more significant for you?'

EASTER DAY

Dawn appearance

St Matthew 28.1 (NEB) *'It was about daybreak on Sunday.'*

INTRODUCTION

Daybreak on Sunday differs for most of us from any other day in the week. It is the day when most people, if wakened by the dawn chorus of birds or young children, turn over in bed with no immediate need to get up. There is something different about Sunday morning for those who rise to go to church; the stillness of the early morning. It was in no sense a day of rest for the womenfolk making their way to the tomb that Easter morn; the Sabbath was over and another working week had begun. So early in the morning there may not yet have been much evidence of the rush and bustle of the daily round; but their hearts were far from being still and quiet.

They came prepared

They had themselves prepared spices and aromatic oils so that they may perform this last loving service for their friend and Master. They came prepared to take any consequences of being discovered at the tomb and recognised as associates of Jesus the Nazarene who had been put to death two days earlier. They came expecting to face the problem of moving the stone which blocked the entrance to the grave. They came in love; but troubled in thought and spirit.

They were astonished

On arrival at the garden cemetery they were astonished to find the stone rolled away. Their astonishment turned to amazement and fear when they saw sitting on the stone an 'angel of the Lord' (St Matthew 28.2). They were more astonished at the message which he gave them.

They were confronted

Astonished, amazed and filled with awe; if this message is true what unspeakable joy if he is risen. 'Suddenly Jesus was there in their path' (St Matthew 28.9). No chance of avoiding him: there he was, confirming the directive of the angel. The message contained the good news: 'Jesus is Risen.' Jesus gave them assurance: 'Do not be afraid'. Jesus gave the command 'go and give this news to my disciples'.

APPLICATION

More than usual have this Sunday risen from their beds and come to church to make their Easter communion. Your presence this Easter Day witnesses to your belief that 'Christ is Risen'. Our belief that Christ rose on the third day is based on evidence other than the discovery of an empty tomb; which is not mentioned in the Epistles. The Resurrection appearances and the vitality of the early church are the positive evidence; but when the Gospels came to be written each contained a narrative of the empty tomb. Note this: 'Suddenly Jesus was in their path', an unexpected resurrection appearance, his first, but not without warning. Although they did not know it, they had been prepared for this encounter by the angel who had reminded them: 'He has been raised from the dead, as he said he would be'. Are we prepared for an encounter with the Risen Lord? The encounter is here in this church on this altar this Easter morning. Have we come lovingly to expect him to be here in his Risen presence? If we have we shall not only see him we shall receive him.

THE SUNDAY AFTER EASTER

The Bread of Life

St John 6.35 (NEB) *'I am the bread of life.'*

INTRODUCTION

If you were asked 'What is a parable?', what answer would you give? Doubtless you would give an example, such as the sower and the seed, the Good Samaritan or the Prodigal Son. They would have this in common: they are stories told by Jesus which contain a spiritual meaning, if only we can discern it. They are indeed one of the most distinctive features of Christ's teaching. You may, therefore, be surprised to learn that no parables are recorded in the Fourth Gospel. There are, however, seven 'I am' sayings of Jesus of a similar character; that is, you have to possess the 'key' to discover their hidden meaning. William Temple suggests that the first of these seven sayings gives a clue to the whole series, 'which represents the appropriation of what is offered by God objectively and externally so that it becomes subjective and inward power; that is the sacramental principle'.*

Let me remind you of these sayings or parables (the term the Archbishop uses) and the developing thought which underlies the series:

(1) *'I am the bread of life.'* Christ nourishes us and gives us strength.

(2) *'I am the light of the world'* (St John 8.12). Jesus gives us light to show the way we should follow in that strength.

(3) *'I am the door of the sheepfold'* (St John 10.7). He is himself the entrance into the fellowship of life.

(4) *'I am the good shepherd'* (St John 10.11). Christ is the guardian of that fellowship, who by his sacrifice wins new members for it.

*William Temple, *Readings in St John's Gospel* (St Martin's Library edition) 1963. p. 77.

(5) *'I am the resurrection and I am life'* (St John 11.25). Jesus is himself the life of that fellowship, which lives by him alone.

(6) *'I am the real vine'* (St John 15.1). Christ is even the fellowship, for its members are incorporated into him, and it is his life which vitalises them.

(7) *'I am the way; I am the truth and I am life'* (St John 14.6). Comprehensively, Jesus is himself the way to be followed in action, the truth to be believed, the life to be lived.

On these four Sundays after Easter we are invited to reflect and pray on four of these themes in the light of our Easter faith—The Bread of Life, The Good Shepherd, The Resurrection and the Life, and The Way, the Truth and the Life.

APPLICATION

'I am the bread of life' gives us the clue to this series of sayings. Before we receive the sacramental bread of life in this eucharist we shall pray, *'Give us this day our daily bread'*. This at once indicates God's concern with our physical needs; indeed the bread which we offer for use at this eucharist acknowledges our dependence upon God and man's labour. Dependence upon the Creator and the labour of many in the provision of the bread—the farmer, the industrialists who manufacture farm machinery, the chain of exporters and importers, transporters, millers and bakers; and our own work enabling us to buy bread to satisfy our needs. This we offer, God takes and gives to us 'the bread of life'. But note this: 'Give us *this* day our daily bread' whether to satisfy our bodily or spiritual needs. We are not to look back nostalgically to the past or anxiously to the future. This does not mean that we are not to plan for the future; we are not to be anxious. 'Satisfy, O God, our present needs, nourish us and give us strength this day through Jesus, the Bread of Life.'

SECOND SUNDAY AFTER EASTER

Known

St John 10.14 (NEB) '*I am the good shepherd; I know my own sheep and my sheep know me—as the Father knows me and I know the Father—and I lay down my life for the sheep.*'

INTRODUCTION

One of the favourite images we possess of Jesus is that of the good shepherd who laid down his life for the sheep. Let us examine this familiar shepherd image more closely.

I am the good shepherd; I know my own sheep!

Most of us would find it very difficult to distinguish one sheep from another; lambs frisking around in the spring look very much alike and we probably wonder how they find their own mother. The shepherd knows his *own* sheep and has no difficulty in distinguishing one from the other. It is not just a matter of appearances; the shepherd knows the differing temperaments and habits of his sheep—his sheep, mind you, his *own* sheep, those for which he has a responsibility of guardianship. This is what distinguishes the good shepherd from the hireling. '*I am the good shepherd; my sheep know me.*' Familiarity and trust bring knowledge. The sheep get to know the shepherd's habits, the slightest inflexion of the voice indicating whether he is approving or disapproving of the sheep's behaviour. Perhaps they could distinguish him by his appearance, certainly they would know him for his constant and reliable care.

I am the good shepherd; I lay down my life for the sheep

Isn't this taking things a bit too far? Is the good shepherd crazy in going to this extreme to save his sheep? Surely human life is more important than silly, stupid sheep? The hireling surely had more common sense. He ran away when the wolf came; saved his own skin rather than that of the sheep. Anyone hearing this

47

saying of Jesus and unaware of its context and hidden meaning, might well reason along those lines. But you and I know that there is a paschal significance behind the saying, 'I lay down my life for the sheep'; referring as it does to the death of Christ on the cross of Calvary, that we might have life and have it more abundantly.

The ideal relationship is indicated in the phrase, 'as the Father knows me and I know the Father'. We are taken as we are, with all our blemishes and peculiarities and we are known. Is this not a comforting thought, that being one amongst many who are his own by baptism and incorporation into the Body of Christ, yet he knows all about me, accepts me and cares about me as an individual? We are known as individuals; remember the shepherd who sought the lost sheep. We can be foolish and not respond. How well do we know Jesus? Jesus said, 'If you know me you would know my Father too'. (St John 14.7).

THIRD SUNDAY AFTER EASTER

Alive in Christ

St John 11.26 (NEB) *'If a man has faith in me, even though he die, he shall come to life: and no one who is alive and has faith shall ever die.'*

INTRODUCTION

Today's gospel tells only part of a gospel incident; A friend of Jesus, Lazarus the brother of Mary and Martha had died.

Lazarus decays

'Lazarus had already been four days in the tomb.' Bodily decay had already begun. Anything that Jesus might do for him involved far more than resuscitation of a lifeless body.

Jesus delays

Why did Jesus not come at once when he received the message? Did he not love this family dearly? Were they not to be numbered among his closest friends? Recollect another occasion when the crowds followed Jesus and the question arose how they were to be fed. These words appear in the narrative: 'Jesus himself knew what he meant to do' (St John 6.6). Jesus knew what he would do on this occasion, and it is not unreasonable to conclude that Jesus delayed his coming so as to strengthen the faith of the bereaved sisters and eventually to reward them with the joy of having their brother restored to them.

Mary stays

It was four days after the funeral had taken place. The grief of bereavement had so impinged upon the lives of the family that they might well have been dead. Even the news that Jesus was coming could not rouse Mary from her self-enforced seclusion. Life must go on; but not for her; all that made life worth living had been destroyed by this one experience. This is not an uncommon experience for us; the grief of mourning can be so catastrophic for us as to make the bereaved 'dead' though physically alive.

Martha's faith

Today's gospel recalls the conversation which Martha had with Jesus when she met him. These points are worth noting: firstly, belief in a general resurrection is expressed, reminding us that human hopes of a resurrection ante-date the resurrection of Jesus on Easter Day; secondly, Jesus states: 'I am the resurrection and I am life. If a man has faith in me, even though he die, he shall come to life; and no one who is alive and has faith shall ever die' (St John 11.25, 26); thirdly, Martha's confession of faith precedes the raising of Lazarus from the tomb. (This is perhaps why the gospel lectionary for today stops short at this expression of faith in Jesus.)

49

What does it mean to be alive? Decay does not necessarily await the occurrence of death. We have only to visit a geriatric ward and see men and women who though physically alive in all other respects are 'dead'. This does raise an acute question— is the prolongation of existence by modern drugs (as distinct from definite ending of life) a Christian act? Except for relief of pain why give a person antibiotics to cure pneumonia merely to enable them to continue a cabbage-like existence in a geriatric ward?

Until there is an active response of the will to the love of God by anyone bereaved, it might well be said that they are more dead than alive but what do we mean by being alive in Christ? Harry Williams has reminded us that true resurrection can be a living experience—a renewal of body, mind and spirit.*

FOURTH SUNDAY AFTER EASTER

Spiritual safari

> St John 14.6 (NEB) '*I am the way; I am the truth and I am life; no man comes to the Father except by me.*'

INTRODUCTION

Among the many holiday brochures which seek to entice us year by year there can usually be found one which claims to satisfy the needs of the more adventurous—'Why not join us on a safari over the Sahara?' Certainly a holiday with a difference and not one which panders to our creature comforts. Nevertheless a more comfortable safari than many a trader, colonial officer or missionary made when the continent of Africa was being opened up by adventurous Europeans. Then, as now, if the safari is a long one there will be several resting-places. Indeed as colonial government spread, at each and every station

* H. A. Williams: *The True Resurrection*, Mitchell Beazley, 1972.

there was built a rest-house to accommodate official and non-official visitors. Each rest-house being staffed with a cook-cum-houseboy, who notified in advance to expect occupants for the night should have had the place all ready, the bath-water hot, and food and drink for the travellers. Before this more permanent network was established it was necessary to send someone on ahead to prepare for when the main party arrived.

The evening that Jesus gave his final discourse to his disciples they had travelled but a little way; perhaps only from a village near Jerusalem. Nevertheless preparations had to be made to keep the Passover and Jesus sent on two disciples to get all things ready for the feast. After supper he began to speak of another journey, one which he will make alone, a spiritual journey to the Father.

The Way

The Way was one which disturbed the disciples. Jesus spoke of the Way of the Cross. What was even more disturbing Jesus not only announced that one of the inner band would betray him; he told Peter that before the cock crowed next morning, he would deny him. For three years they had been everywhere with Jesus and then he told them he must make *this* journey alone. It was not until after the Resurrection that they understood that this was the Way of Love.

The Truth

The Truth is that God is Love. Love is no abstract theory; it can only be related to and experienced by persons. God is a personal being and in order that men might begin to know this, he expressed what is personal (love) in a person, Jesus Christ. 'Truth', said William Temple, 'is the perfect correlation of mind and reality; and this is actualised in the Lord's Person.'*

The Life

Those who seek the excitement of the twentieth-century safari doubtless are seeking after *life*. If we really want the vitalising

*William Temple, *Readings in St John's Gospel* (St Martin's Library edition) 1963. p. 222.

energy of all that lives we can find the source in Jesus. Even though we may not always recognise him as the source of life; he is the well-spring of such vitality to possess. Remember the water of life which he offered to the woman of Samaria.

APPLICATION

'No man comes to the Father except by me.' Jesus has left us in no doubt. Each life is an individual spiritual safari to the Father. On this spiritual pilgrimage Jesus calls us to an ever greater perfection in and through him. The resting-place which he has gone on to prepare for us we may expect to be a series of resting-places on the journey; times of refreshment and renewal. At each resting-place Jesus is there to welcome us when exhausted, and by his aid we overcome the obstacles which cause us to stumble and fall. He, who stumbled and fell under the weight of the cross, is there to pick us up and set us again on our way to greater perfection on the Christian pilgrimage which is our spiritual safari.

FIFTH SUNDAY AFTER EASTER

Going to the Father

St John 16.17 (NEB) *'Because I am going to the Father.'*

INTRODUCTION

It was only in the light and experience of the Resurrection of Jesus that the disciples understood the implications of his farewell discourses. It is only in the light and knowledge of Christ's Resurrection and Ascension that we can begin to appreciate the relevance of this saying of Jesus which initially caused such concern to the disciples: 'What does he mean by . . . "I am going to the Father"?' In the fullness of the gospel there is a tremendous depth of meaning in this saying of Jesus.

How was he going to the Father? Like the prodigal son Jesus desired to return to the Father. Unlike the prodigal son he had lived a life of loving obedience to the Father's will. To the amazement of his contemporaries he had demonstrated that God can be approached as a loving Father. He had encouraged a people who were historically and theologically conditioned never to mention the name of God, to dare to address God as '*Abba*, Father'. He had shown what God is like by his own life and ministry. But he was going to the Father in and through three tremendous moments of history which had a future significance for his disciples and all Christians who in succeeding centuries have acknowledged Christ as Lord. A moment of victory achieved on the cross of Calvary; a significant moment on Easter Day, the Resurrection by which we know of his victory; and a triumphant moment, the demonstration of his kingship at his Ascension. He went to the Father to share in the glory of God; that glory which he had temporarily laid aside.

The Ascension of Jesus marks not the end, but the beginning of his going to the Father. His going to the Father is an act which continues throughout time. Do we not believe that he intercedes for us? We address our prayers to God the Father through the Son. He goes to the Father to present us as adopted sons able to benefit only through what he has done and is doing for us. He goes to the Father, with the express promise that God will send another advocate. He goes to the Father praying for the faithfulness of those to whom he has entrusted the furtherance of his work in the Church. He goes to the Father praying for succeeding generations of Christians; all those who believe in him whom they have not seen.

APPLICATION

We are all going to the Father. As prodigal sons our going to the Father is only possible through Christ's going to the Father and the manner of his going. Like the prodigal son we shall be amazed by the generosity of our loving Father.

SIXTH SUNDAY AFTER EASTER

Fulfilment

St Luke 24.44 (JB) '*This is what I meant when I said,
while I was still with you, that everything written about me
in the Law of Moses, in the Prophets and in the Psalms, has
to be fulfilled.*'

INTRODUCTION

Shakespeare and Cranmer might be more surprised and
bewildered by changes in the English language than any other
changes in our society and land which they would find should
they return to England in the twentieth century. Cranmer, for
instance, would be surprised to learn that today the word 'prevent' means 'to stop' and not 'to go before' as he used the word
in one of the prayer-book collects. Shakespeare would be surprised at the development of the English language, particularly
in response to the demands of the technological age. However,
there can still be difficulty in communication even where there
is a common language and culture. On many occasions, without
much success, Jesus had tried to bring his disciples to a full and
adequate understanding of what was meant by his Messiahship.
On the Mount of Transfiguration three of them had witnessed
the vision of his fulfilment; and yet they did not understand.
In the Upper Room and in the Garden of Gethsemane he tried
to convey to them how he was to fulfil his Messianic role. And
now again, in his last instructions, after his Resurrection 'he
opened their minds to understand the scriptures' (St Luke
24.45), as he had done on the walk to Emmaus to two disciples
on the way.

Fulfilment of the Law

Law is necessary to human societies so that men can live together
in harmony. It is ultimately concerned with people and their
relationships. The Law of Moses embraced human relationships
and relationship to God. The new commandment which Jesus

gave to his disciples and his earlier emphasis on the first commandment to love God indicates the relationship which should exist and which the Torah sought to ensure. Positive law and prohibitive regulations only exist because men do not live up to the ideal relationship to God and their fellow men. Jesus was the fulfilment of the Law through the perfection of his life and love; his love of God fulfilled in perfect obedience, enabling him to show his love for man through his compassion and his Passion.

Fulfilment of the prophets

'Thus saith the Lord'; the prophets were in no doubt that they were entrusted with a message from God. A message usually appropriate to a specific occasion frequently with reference to a political and social situation, apparently contrary to the covenant relationship between God and his people. Jesus condemned the political and social situation of his day in words and by action. People were amazed at his authority. But the fulfilment of the prophetic in Jesus is to be seen not so much in what he said and did as in the nature of the authority which he claimed.

Fulfilment of the Psalms

We are familiar with Christ as the fulfilment of the Law and the Prophets, but what of the Psalms? Is there any human experience and emotion that is not to be found expressed in the Psalms? Jesus experienced human emotions and situations to the full; the Psalms also indicate his unique fulfilment as the Lamb of God who takes away the sin of the world.

APPLICATION

Every person at birth inherits a life of fulfilment. To what extent will that life be fulfilled? Political and social situations will help determine this and psychological and emotional make-up will influence it. Christian fulfilment must be in accord with the Law of God. Fulfilment through faith in Christ must find expression in social and political situations with a fearless Christian witness enlivened by a compassion for all people. Fulfilment for the Christian has to be aimed at in all human situations and emotions and this can only be possible through the Love of God and our conviction that this is so.

PENTECOST

Power and peace

St John 14.27 (JB)
'Peace I bequeath to you,
my own peace I give you,
a peace the world cannot give, this is my gift to you.
Do not let your hearts be troubled or afraid.'

INTRODUCTION

There is little doubt that power is something to be reckoned with in our time. World powers have waged two catastrophic wars and seldom does a year go by without some military confrontation in some part of the world. Nuclear power has brought a new dimension to warfare. Political power can display a variety of attitudes towards those governed; and in the traditional democratic societies political authority is now questioned and power groups of one kind or another threaten the established government. Black Power is expressive of the confrontation between black and white peoples. Economic power is increasingly exerted between two apparently opposing groups: management increasingly in the hands of greater and more powerful units or combines; and workers militant in their trade unions. Power can be asserted by one person over others. The schoolchildren's revolt is a demonstration against the power of the teacher and the unrepresentative structure of school government. Women's lib expresses dissatisfaction with male dominance in so many spheres. Power is exerted in these and other ways for one or other of the following purposes: *entrenchment*, to make certain that there is no deterioration in the present power position, to hold on to our control at all costs;

containment, to ensure that structures stay as they are; *advancement*, to achieve some breakthrough in the power structure to one's own advantage. Power exerted in any of these ways demonstrates the exercise of self-will to self-advantage, no wonder that Jesus said that there is 'a peace the world cannot give'.

It is within the context of our power-structures and struggles for power that Jesus bequeaths his own peace. A peace so powerful and real that hearts need not be troubled or afraid. Within living memory the exercise of power reached its most abhorrent manifestation in Nazi Germany; and yet we find even in those conditions there were some who discovered the inward peace of Jesus, as they lived through the agonies and deprivations of imprisonment and torture. Read Bonhoeffer's *Letters and Papers from Prison*. What do you make of a man whose own doom was sealed and who yet could write this:

> 'I am still discovering, right up to this moment, that it is only by living completely in this world that one learns to have faith. One must completely abandon any attempt to make something of oneself. . . . By this-worldliness I mean living unreservedly in life's duties, problems, successes and failures, experiences and perplexities. In so doing we throw ourselves into the arms of God, taking seriously not our own suffering, but those of God in the world . . . . How can success make us arrogant, or failure lead us astray, when we share in God's sufferings through a life of this kind?'*

Here was a man responsive to the power of God which brings peace which passes our understanding.

APPLICATION

Pentecost is concerned with power; the power of the Holy Spirit which transformed the disciples. This same power can transform us so that we do not seek personal power or privileged position. The power of the Holy Spirit can give us an inward

---

*Quoted in D. L. Edwards: *Religion and Change*, Hodder and Stoughton, 1969. p. 366.

peace in the midst of the power-complex in which we have to live out our lives in obedience to God's will. Thus our hearts need not be troubled nor afraid. Such is the gift of pentecostal power.

THE SUNDAY AFTER PENTECOST
(Trinity Sunday)

What is God like?

St Matthew 11.27 (JB) *'No one knows the Father except the Son and those to whom the Son chooses to reveal him.'*

INTRODUCTION

A child's question, 'What is God like?' causes us great consternation. How shall we answer it? There is the communication problem of the child's maturity and understanding. Then there is the deeper question, 'What is God really like?' This is a question which has exercised the mind of man throughout history and a variety of answers have been made from tribal dieties to modern theologians speaking of 'being in depth'.

Christian understanding must begin with the revelation of God in the Old Testament and how the chosen people came to understand what God was like through their relationship and experiences. There is a sense in which they regarded Jehovah as father of the Jewish nation and of Israel as a people. Theirs was a growing knowledge of God and when they became a nation with a monarch, God was then regarded as the father of the king. 'I will be his Father and he shall be my son' (2 Samuel 7.14). With this exception the Fatherhood of God is never individualised; although God is father of the nation and of the king, in the Old Testament he is never said to be the father of an individual man or woman. In such an understanding it is possible for there to be an unbridgeable gap between God and man. This was expressed in the concept of 'holiness'—God the 'wholly other', the 'separate'. Associated attributes are the unconditional authority of God and his almighty power.

'No one knows the Father except the Son'; this accounts for the distinctive revealing of God's nature by Jesus of God the Father. When a child asks 'What is God like?', can we use the word 'Father' in our answer? This will depend a very great deal upon the personal experience of the child in relationship to his own father. It is possible for a man to be father of a child as physically responsible for the child's existence and for him not to have any further relationship with the child. But the fatherhood of God, as Jesus revealed it, is a relationship of love, care and intimacy, a close bond of love, sympathy and friendship. This is demonstrated in the relationship of God and Jesus, 'No one knows the Son except the Father, just as no one knows the Father but the Son'.

APPLICATION

It is possible for us to know the Father. Jesus went on to say that the same relationship is possible for 'those to whom the Son chooses to reveal him'. Jesus reveals the Father through his own life of loving obedience to the will of God. Jesus teaches what God is like in the parables; though their meaning may be hid from the clever and wise. Jesus reveals to us what God is like through prayer: the fellowship of prayer in his own example and the pattern of prayer given us in the Lord's Prayer. There is a prior condition to our understanding and receiving of the revelation, we need to possess a simple childlike trust in the revealer himself. We shall then be receptive to the deeper understanding and experience of God given by the Holy Spirit. This is really what The Trinity is all about; it is a living experience, not a theological dogma!

SECOND SUNDAY AFTER PENTECOST

The right use of resources

St Luke 14.17 (NEB) *'Please come, everything is now ready.'*

INTRODUCTION

We should consider it very bad taste and be most offended if people invited to dinner made excuses when all was ready. But how do *we* react to God's abundant provision of resources from man's use? 'Please come, everything is now ready.' Consider this as the privilege granted by God to the human race to be custodians of the resources of the world in which we live. God has given man a share in creative activity, the freedom and ability to develop skills and techniques. How does he use them?

The man of possessions, property and power

'I have bought myself a piece of land, and I must go and look after it' (St Luke 14.18). For what purposes? Is it unjust to see this manifested today at its worst in land speculation? Manipulation of resources and manpower to what end? Or again take the persuasiveness of advertising—the hidden persuaders possessing our very minds and wills (if you think this an exaggeration read Vance Packard's *The Hidden Persuaders*) to add to their property and their possessions. So powerful is advertising that many luxuries in our homes today are regarded as essentials by us. Consider *your* standard of living and reflect that the greater part of mankind is on the poverty line or below it. With all the world's resources and the skills of this technological age is this stewardship of resources?

The man of work and productivity

'I have bought five yoke of oxen, and I am on my way to try them out' (St Luke 14.19). What is he going to do with them? What kind of industry and productivity? It is easy to criticise those responsible for producing pornography, sex and violence in films and literature; what about those industries where disposability ends in another sort of pollution? Consider the behaviour of organised labour in strikes, go-slows, absenteeism, etc. Is this stewardship of natural resources, capital equipment and manpower? Where does the Christian employer and employee stand in all this?

The man who is creative

'I have just got married, and for that reason I cannot come.' Many newly married couples in their wedded happiness find they have no need of others, nor to find enjoyment and satisfaction in outside interests: yes, so-called true love can be selfish. All married couples must now exercise a responsible attitude towards society through family planning. The Christian churches do not speak with a united voice on this issue; but where do Christians stand in relation to family planning and contraception?

APPLICATION

Many issues have been raised in this sermon taking as an introductory basis the three excuses made in the story which Jesus told about the invitees to a dinner who did not come. The issues raised relate to property and power, productivity and labour, family life and family planning. There is no doubt that Christians must exercise responsible stewardship and most of us do. 'Please come, for everything is now ready', does not mean that the resources are limitless. Indeed there are some prophets of doom. In the exercise of responsibility there is only one way; to begin with ourselves and not to make excuses.

THIRD SUNDAY AFTER PENTECOST

Requests answered

St Luke 8.41, 44 (NEB) '*Throwing himself down at Jesus'
feet he begged him to come to his house . . . . She came up
behind and touched the edge of his cloak.*'

INTRODUCTION

We are accustomed to television commentators analysing
events. Often we find ourselves making a similar approach,
forgetful that people are involved. Let us this morning try to
concentrate on three people involved in today's gospel, con-
centrating our thoughts on them.

The woman suffering from haemorrhages for twelve years

Perhaps the women listening to this sermon can best appreciate
her plight. Her illness was menorrhagia, a continuous men-
struation. Consider how distressing and debilitating its effects
must have been. We can imagine her anxiety; and in our
imagination we can see her going to this or that doctor,
trying every kind of cure; all without success for a period of
twelve years. The psychological effects were heightened by
the Levitical provision which declared her permanently unclean,
unfit for any human contact. Thus furtively, though prayerfully,
she dared to touch the hem of Jesus' garment.

Jairus

The gospels do not name the twelve-year-old who was miraculously restored to life. She and her mother are introduced into
the narrative at the end. Our attention is purposefully drawn to
Jairus. He was one of the leaders of the local synagogue; the
president of the local council of elders. It required courage and
humility on his part to come to Jesus. Courage because of the
rising tide of official disapproval of Jesus' ministry. Humility
because in coming to Jesus he acknowledges publicly his faith

in the power of Jesus; thus acknowledging Jesus. He comes in prayer throwing himself down at the feet of Jesus.

Jesus

Jesus answered their requests beyond their expectations. The woman was not allowed to escape without a public declaration of what she had done. If she had slipped away, she might well have had a feeling of guilt, having broken the law of unclean-ness. It was a serious offence for her to have touched Jesus, because the law implied that some of her uncleanness passed to the person touched. Also she had gained her cure by a stealthy action. Jesus showed her that her new health was not due to magical powers, but to her own faith in the saving activity of God. Thus she gained not only a physical cure, she entered into a fuller life under the grace and the fatherhood of God. Jairus' steadfast faith was rewarded by restoration even from death; a greater answer than he could ever have anticipated to his prayers.

APPLICATION

Do you believe that every prayer is answered? When we pray 'according to thy will' we are sometimes doubtful that there has been an answer because the answer is not that which we want. God always answers prayer in one of three ways: yes, no, wait! His purpose is to enable us more fully to be dependent upon him, to increase our faith; so that we can have a richer and more abundant life under his grace. God's answer is in judge-ment and mercy; he knows what is appropriate to our every situation and condition, as he did for Jairus and the woman suffering from menorrhagia.

FOURTH SUNDAY AFTER PENTECOST

Each one matters

St Luke 15.10 (NEB) '*I tell you, there is joy among the angels of God over one sinner who repents.*'

INTRODUCTION

We live in a welfare state and possess many benefits therefrom. Yet the vast problem of dealing with the health and well-being of the whole nation has created 'built-in' problems. When dealing with whole groups, old age pensioners, widows, children's milk; the approach tends to become impersonal. When we go to the hospital we sometimes feel that we are 'just another case' identified by a code number on a card or a 'time-slot' in an appointments book. The system can be impersonal. When we go out shopping it is more often to a chain store or supermarket where each customer is another 'unit of sale' passing through a check-point. I am one of the masses for whom the mass-media caters in our leisure hours; and mass-media advertising tends to make us all eat, drink and dress in the same fashion. Doesn't anybody care for me?

Fortunately, yes! There is much loving service in the hospitals and other agencies of the welfare-state. This is supplemented by voluntary effort such as the Samaritans, marriage guidance counsellors. Christian politicians are to be found coping with problems at local and national levels. There are some television directors not prepared to be governed by what appeals to the masses. But who cares for me in the most important state of my life, my relationship to God?

APPLICATION

Jesus told the parables of the lost sheep and the lost coin in reply to criticism that he associated with tax-gatherers and sinners. The significance is to be found in the joy 'over one sinner who repents'. (St Luke 15.7). Is there one of us who is not a sinner? We should notice a factor common to both parables:

the lost sheep was one which already belonged to the fold, the lost coin had already been in the woman's possession. How effective are our local pastoral arrangements to notice who has gone missing, to discover why and to bring back into the fold just one person? Statistics show us a trend of those who belong to the fold through baptism and do not come forward to confirmation; or being confirmed no longer make their communion. The devil so bemuses us with statistics that we are hindered from recognising the need to look for the one sheep, the child of God behind the statistic. To all who have strayed we can acknowledge that we are also sinners and that each one matters. God has given us a priesthood with unique power to pronounce absolution and forgiveness in his name. In preaching we witness to the gospel of God's reconciliation. Each one matters in God's sight; let us see to it that each one matters in this church.

FIFTH SUNDAY AFTER PENTECOST

All people matter

St Luke 17.11 (NEB) '*In the course of his journey to Jerusalem he was travelling through the borderlands of Samaria and Galilee.*'

INTRODUCTION

Jesus was travelling through the borderlands of Samaria and Galilee, but there was more than geographical boundaries which separated the Jews and the Samaritans; an enmity existed, based upon prejudices embedded in their cultures over the centuries. Jesus demonstrated that there were no barriers of race or class in the kingdom of God. He offered living water to the woman of Samaria, a Samaritan was among the ten lepers who were cleansed and the good Samaritan was cited as an example of true neighbourliness.

Are there any barriers to be broken down today? Two examples will suffice to show that all people matter in the sight of God.

(1) *Race*

The race problem is assuming a new role in many parts of the world. The days are past when all that seemed necessary was to get white people and black people to be kind to each other; this can now be interpreted as white supremacy or paternalism. Today we see black people who will not tolerate white domination any longer, there is seething unrest as they seek liberation. 'Why shouldn't we fight for our liberation?' they ask, 'You fought in Europe to liberate people from the domination of Hitler'. Sometimes the reasons for conflict exist independent of the colour of skin; job shortages and housing shortages provide avenues for conflict among people of the same colour. What would Jesus have to say about this problem of race? Where and how should the church take a firm stand? We well know Christians will not speak with a united voice on this issue, nevertheless these are questions which we cannot avoid answering.

(2) *Politics*

Many problems associated with race are due to conditions of want or unfavourable economic and social conditions or a feeling of inferior status. In this country we would probably claim that a democratic government seeks to care for the welfare of all. The acts of any government, democratic or otherwise, need to be judged by Christian principles which precede democratic and modern forms of government by many centuries. Michael Ramsey has recently reminded us:

> 'Some of the basic Christian principles, I would describe as pre-political rather than as political. For instance, I do not think it can be said that democracy or majority rule as such is a Christian principle: and we remember that Christ sometimes showed

contempt for the views of majorities. What is however a Christian principle is the right of every person created in God's image to the full realisation of his powers of mind and body, and this includes full and free citizenship with democracy as a corollary.'*

(3) *All people matter*

Last week we saw that each one matters and that there is a special Christian responsibility to each individual Christian. Christ saves us, not to live out our lives in a vacuum, but in the world. Christians must apply their Christian principles to the affairs of men knowing that to God all people matter and that through Christ's redemptive act all barriers are broken.

SIXTH SUNDAY AFTER PENTECOST

Is our Church blind?

> St Mark 10.46 (NEB) '*As he was leaving the town, with his disciples and a large crowd, Bartimaeus son of Timaeus, a blind beggar, was seated at the roadside.*'

INTRODUCTION

Bartimaeus, though blind, had the vision to appreciate that Jesus could help him. Possessing our sight we may lack spiritual vision to discern God's purposes today. The Church even may be blind to the light of the Spirit or the vision of God. Is our Church blind? Let us try and assess our position as the local Church here. We do not necessarily need to follow 'St Withits': but there is perhaps a danger in being like 'St Conservatives'. Like Bartimaeus we must recognise our need, we must pray, we must answer Christ's call and we must walk by faith.

*Michael Ramsey: *The Christian Priest Today*, SPCK. 1972. pp. 37, 38.

It seems to me that Christ is calling the Church to a new vision through the challenge of those who do not find the institutional Church answering their needs or their understanding of the vision of Christ. They are critical of our worship that it has no meaning for them. They find the structures of the Church inappropriate to the twentieth century. Above all they claim that we do not live up to our profession of Christians.

Worship

The Liturgical Commission has challenged us with new services which have been authorised for experimental use by the General Synod and may be used locally with the agreement of the PCC. How have *we* used this opportunity? 'St Conservatives' have remained faithful to 1662, their main consideration being those who regularly worship there. Is there not a danger that the beauty and familiarity of the Prayer Book language can blind us to their meaning? I am not concerned with the few words which have changed their meaning (such as *prevent*). Compare the Confession at the eucharist in 1662 with that in Series 3 and see the directness of the latter. Should we not also bear in mind those who are visitors, the young and those entering a church for the first time? Two important considerations must determine our action: which service is appropriate to *our* needs here? How effectively do we present our services?

Structures

For centuries the Church Militant relied upon the parochial strategy of an incumbent and two churchwardens to be the effective force. No wonder that we seem to be on the defensive, rather than the offensive in our warfare for Christ. For fifty years we have had the Church Assembly and PCC's; now we have synodical government. But this is not the effective structure for mission in the parish. What about house communions? What about discussion groups, no not group dynamics but searching the scriptures? Thinking and praying about the structure for mission raises the question of the ministry of the church. Is Christ calling you to serve him in the ministry? Are we being called to visualise and use new patterns of local ministry? What sort of ministry is suitable for this parish?

The blind man restored to sight is a new man. The church with a new vision, flooded with the light of Christ, can become a new community.

SEVENTH SUNDAY AFTER PENTECOST

Cross-examined

St Mark 12.28 (NEB) *'Then one of the lawyers, who had been listening to these discussions and had noted how well he answered, came forward and asked him, "Which commandment is first of all?"'*

INTRODUCTION

The witness entered the witness-box, took the oath and was questioned by the prosecution lawyer; his testimony was vital to the conviction of the man on trial. He answered clearly and without hesitation the questions put to him by learned counsel. But then the defence counsel rose, holding a sheaf of papers in his left hand and his gown by the right, he began questioning the witness. How would he stand up to the cross-examination? Cross-examination which is so vital a procedure in the administering of justice.

Jesus often found himself being questioned and cross-examined. The Pharisees and the Herodians had on this occasion first tried to trap him, 'Are we or are we not permitted to pay taxes to the Roman Emperor? Shall we pay or not?' (St Mark 12.14). The Sadducees (who said that there is no resurrection) then came into the attack with a question about a woman who, in turn, had married seven brothers. 'At the resurrection, when they come back to life, whose wife will she be, since all seven had married her?' Jesus confounded them with his answers to these questions.

Listening to these discussions was a lawyer who had been impressed by the answers which Jesus had just given. We can imagine this lawyer anxious to come to the defence of Jesus in cross-examination. Certainly he gave Jesus the opportunity to display his orthodoxy when he asked, 'Which commandment is first of all?' Jesus gave the correct answer and received due praise from the lawyer, who went on to express learned opinion that to love God and your neighbour as yourself 'is far more than any burnt-offering or sacrifices'. (St Mark 12.33).

APPLICATION

Imagine yourself on trial for your Christian beliefs. You have carefully built up your evidence to support your faith. Then you face cross-examination knowing full well that every legal ploy will be used to undermine your confidence. How would you answer the opening question 'The traditional summary of the law, is it binding on us today?' It was the Law given to Moses, 'Hear, O Israel'. It was law appropriate to the chosen people living under a covenant-relationship with Jehovah. Since then mankind has been cross-examined and saved on Calvary. Here is the one oblation, once offered, a full, perfect and sufficient sacrifice. By this same act a new covenant was made and we are the New Israel. The two-fold summary, to love God and our neighbour does apply.

More important than defending our faith is how we live up to the fulfilment of Christ's commands. Will Jesus say to us, 'You are not far from the kingdom of God'? (St Mark 12.34).

EIGHTH SUNDAY AFTER PENTECOST

Love your enemies

St Luke 6.28 (NEB) *'Love your enemies.'*

INTRODUCTION

Only three words in our text, but they need careful consideration if we are to appreciate and follow our Lord's teaching: 'Love your enemies'.

Your

The easiest of the words to define is 'your'. In the context of Christ's speaking to his contemporary hearers and to us, 'your' includes all men and women who hear or read these words. 'Your' includes you and me.

Enemies

It is perhaps unfortunate that no lawyer asked Jesus the question, 'And who is your enemy?' If, however, we examine the possible range of our enemies we may better understand the meaning of Christian love.

The enemy may be another nation. When Jesus spoke these words the Jews were living in an enemy-occupied country and this was perhaps the interpretation that his hearers put upon the words, 'love your enemies'. The enemy in this sense is not one of our own individual making or choice we are involved because of our nationality and our government's decision to go to war.

The enemy may be the other side in employment. Certainly in the confrontation between management and trade unions which now is a feature of our industrial and economic life, the 'them' and 'us' attitude hardens into opposing positions of strength.

The enemy may be society and its divisions. Some people start off with greater initial advantages in life. The family into which a child is born may give a better start in life. Recent research shows that children of working-class families have already lost a position in the educational process by the age of seven. This sort of situation can mean that we hate those who have advantages over us; and hate is a symptom of enmity.

The enemy may be the family. Many married couples seem to live in a state of perpetual warfare. Grievances are enlarged upon, imagination sets to work and living together becomes intolerable. Generation gap covers that wide range of discordant relationships between parents and children.

The enemy is usually myself. We could extend the range of enemies, but in all these cases it is well to remember that we are the enemies of those whom we regard as our enemies. Perhaps the best way to define enmity is to acknowledge that 'anybody or any situation which in my view conflicts with my self-interest' is my enemy. That is, by my very selfish nature I am my own worst enemy.

Love

What interpretation of love is sufficiently comprehensive to deal with such a diversity of possible enemies? Jesus did not tell his disciples to fall in love with their enemies, that is passionate devotion (*eros*) or to feel for them as they felt for their families and friends showing affection (*philia*). Christian love (*agape*) is a gracious, determined and active interest in the true welfare of others; which, if we reflect upon today's gospel, is not deterred by hatred, cursing and abuse, not limited by calculation of deserts or results. It is based solely upon the nature of God; it does not retaliate, it seeks no reward; it is not censorious.

APPLICATION

It is so easy for us to be jealous of fellow-worshippers, who seem to do all the special jobs for the Church, or tenaciously we hold on to a position; thus attitudes may harden. Our attitude towards someone who takes an opposing view on the PCC may affect our relationship with him as a person. If *agape* is not evident within the Body of Christ how can we show our love to outsiders? Archbishop Temple reminds us that 'the Church is unique among the institutions of man in that it exists, not for those who belong to it, but for those who do not'. This is *agape* in action.

NINTH SUNDAY AFTER PENTECOST

Faith and prayer essential

> St Mark 9.14, 28–29 (NEB) '*When they came back to the disciples they saw a large crowd surrounding them and lawyers arguing with them . . . Then Jesus went indoors, and his disciples asked him privately, "Why could we not cast it out?" "There is no means of casting out this sort but prayer".*'

INTRODUCTION

Pick up your *Radio Times* or *TV Times* and you will find a diversity of programmes which do not appear to have any connection with each other at all. However, each channel, anxious to keep you tuned-in to its programmes once you have switched-on, uses the continuity announcer as a linkman, building on to your enjoyment of a programme which you have just seen with an attractive build-up of later programmes in the day, so that you will continue watching that channel.

Although the evangelist has a different objective from entertaining us, he is anxious that we should continue reading his gospel so that we may be responsive to the Christ he proclaims. He uses the device of a continuity announcer as he links one episode with another; although we need to recognise that later editorial additions to the gospels may give an episode a build-up which was not original. The continuity announcer approach can deepen our understanding of particular incidents in the gospels, providing as it does an introductory link and a concluding link which helps explain the incident; this is particularly true of St Mark's account of the cure of the epileptic boy.

The Introductory Link

Peter, James and John (according to the Marcan sequence) had been sharing in the experience of the Transfiguration of our Lord. On the loneliness of the mountain-top they had experienced a spiritual height which they wanted to capture and maintain. They wanted to build three shelters for Jesus, Moses and Elijah. How good it was to be there: but Jesus said, 'No' and they came back with him to join the other disciples. Immediately they were 'down to earth' in the midst of arguments and disputes. So was Jesus, back to the day to day frustrations and challenges of his ministry.

The Concluding Link

After the cure, when they were alone with Jesus the disciples asked why they were unable to cure the boy. His answer was— only possible by prayer; and earlier he had demonstrated the necessity for faith, no matter how small that faith may be. He had delayed the cure to talk with the father and bring his faith to the test. 'If it is possible!' said Jesus, 'Everything is possible to one who has faith'. (St Mark 9.23).

APPLICATION

When Jesus returned to the disciples he found them arguing with lawyers. We are not told what the argument was about; it might well have been why the boy was an epileptic and the disciples were denying the lawyers arguments that it was due to the sins of the parents. So often it is still a temptation for us to argue and discuss, instead of praying and going out to people in their need. Like Peter, James and John we have to go out from the spiritual heights (of this morning's eucharist) to the depths of human encounter, where our faith is put to the test. It is important that we possess a little faith, for this can grow; it is disastrous to lose our faith even though experiences in life threaten our beliefs. We need to depend more upon God and less upon ourselves; this is the way of prayer. Prayer is living all day in faith and reliance upon God; it is much more than words spoken to him.

TENTH SUNDAY AFTER PENTECOST

The host, the guest and the intruder

St Luke 7.36 (NEB) *'One of the Pharisees invited him to eat with him.'*

INTRODUCTION

The host, the guest and the intruder; these are clearly the people who dominate the dinner scene narrated in today's gospel. The other guests and the servants appear as 'extras'.

The Host

Simon was a Pharisee. Why did he invite Jesus to dine with him? Who were the other invited guests? Was this an invitation with an ulterior motive, or was Simon genuinely interested in what Jesus said and did? When Jesus arrived he certainly greeted him as a Rabbi; but then he acted casually towards him in not offering to Jesus the customary gestures: water for the washing of the feet, the conventional greeting and oil for the head. It would seem that Simon was curious to discover whether or not Jesus was a genuine prophet; and he concluded he was not, because he thought Jesus did not recognise the true character of the intruder. To all outward appearances the Host was a highly respected citizen who lived an impeccable life; but Jesus revealed him to be a hard, selfish and unloving man.

The guest

The guest was Jesus, who did not fail to recognise either the host or the intruder as the kind of people they really were, and he dealt with them accordingly. The intruder was forgiven.

The host was made to acknowledge that the one who is forgiven most will love the benefactor most.

The intruder

We might well ask, 'How did an outsider, let alone a prostitute, gain admission to a house where a dinner party was in progress?' It was not uncommon for the doors to be left open to admit all sorts of people, from beggars in search of food to admirers of a teacher in search of intellectual entertainment. Why did she come? Not to solicit, but because she knew that Jesus was there. Perhaps she had heard him speak, and in faith she came, trusting that through him she would be forgiven. She comes lovingly and tearfully to perform those courtesies which Simon, the host, had so rudely omitted. Her faith brings her to Jesus; her love responds to him.

APPLICATION

Why have we come to church this morning? In faith we have come because Jesus is here and our love responds to him. This morning we receive Christ into our lives at this eucharist and we are hosts to him. As Christians we have invited Jesus to be our permanent guest. How do we receive him? Can he permanently dwell in our hearts? This depends upon the extent to which the love of God permeates our whole being; our thoughts and our acts. You see OUR SIN is very much greater and more serious than our sins. For while the opposite of sins (things which we have done we ought not to have done, and things we have left undone which we ought to have done) is good deeds; the opposite of Sin is Love. So we pray for forgiveness and that the love of God may be shed abroad in our hearts.

ELEVENTH SUNDAY AFTER PENTECOST

Christian duty

St Luke 17.10 (NEB) *'We are servants and deserve no credit; we have only done our duty.'*

INTRODUCTION

Future historians looking at the evidence of life in England in the second half of the twentieth century will, I believe, discern a social revolution. Having lived through the period, most of us are not readily aware of the tremendous social changes which have taken place since the end of the Second World War. Technological advances, hire purchase facilities and regular employment for most people, have meant that most families possess a television set, washing machine, dishwasher and a car, material possessions now thought essential, which the previous generation would largely have regarded as luxuries. There is no doubt that there has been a general rise in the standard of living.

Rising prices, however, continually constitute a threat to the accepted standard of living. Sympathy and aid is given generously to victims of floods in Calcutta, the homeless in Britain and so on; but not usually at the expense of our own standard of living. We are an acquisitive society; we are also a competitive society: there is fierce competition for markets and for fair shares in profits. Almost every month a union applies for a new deal for its members, usually expressed as a percentage increase. Others— businessmen, civil servants, shareholders—see to it that they get their salary increase or share in the profits; without so much publicity. Land speculators make immense sums without adding any appreciable contribution or risk or labour. All justify why they are entitled to more. The prevailing outlook is 'What's in it for me?', 'What's my reward?'; little is said about duties and responsibilities. Perhaps I am overstating my case; yet I don't think so: ask any housewife about the standard of goods and the servicing of gadgets in her home.

This kind of outlook contrasts sharply with the saying of Jesus, 'So with you: when you have carried out all your orders, you should say, "We are servants and deserve no credit; we have only done our duty."' This saying, and the parable about the master and slave which precedes it, concerns our Christian servitude. It is a warning against the book-keeping accountability which aims to set up a spiritual credit balance. The demands of God are exacting; but we cannot earn his approval nor put him under an obligation. We can only do our Christian duty, seeking no other reward than knowing that we do his will. The whole idea of merit is to be abandoned in our approach to God.

TWELFTH SUNDAY AFTER PENTECOST

Taste and see

St Matthew 5.13, 14 (NEB) '*You are salt to the world . . . You are light for all the world.*'

INTRODUCTION

Fashions change; for men as well as women. Each season's new designs, changes in the hem-line, introduce another year's mode for the ladies. The latest styles do not necessarily suit all figures and all ages. Hot pants or mini-skirts are suitable for some to display their legs; but disastrous when a woman appears as 'mutton dressed like lamb'. What do we mean when we say that a man or woman has taste? Someone aware of what kind of clothing is suitable to them and who dresses according to the occasion. Financial resources may considerably aid tasteful appearance, although much can be achieved on a limited budget. In male fashions we now have seasonal changes in dress shirts and ties.

Good taste is more than fashion in clothes. It is fundamental to our whole way of life; the things which we do, the words we speak and the company we keep and attract. As Christ's disciples all our lives should be governed by a desire to 'taste and see how glorious the Lord is'. Taste now meaning that which is pleasing to the palate. Jesus gave us an appropriate illustration, 'You are the salt to the world. And if salt becomes tasteless, how is its saltness to be restored? It is good for nothing but to be thrown away and trodden under foot' (St Matthew 5.13). Here is an argument for the quality and permanence of our Christian witness. Without appearing to contradict this saying of Jesus, it is not contrary to our Christian belief to claim that our lives can be renewed; some 'taste' put back. 'O taste and see how glorious the Lord is' in his eucharistic presence today.

All married men will have experienced the problem which confronts their wives whenever they are invited out to a function if it is to be a formal occasion; 'I wonder if they will be wearing long or short dresses?' Or it may be that the concern is just what to wear; facing a wardrobe bulging out with dresses and suits, she says in desperation, 'I've got nothing to wear!' We should rejoice that our wives take pride in their appearance. It would be little use their going to immense trouble in buying clothes and selecting for the occasion if they were not going to be seen by others. Our Christian witness is to be seen by others; not for our own glory but for the glory of God. 'And you . . . must shed light among your fellows, so that . . . they may give praise to your Father in heaven.' (St Matthew 5.16).

APPLICATION

Have we a vision of God? God set upon a hill outside a city wall to draw all men unto himself. How do we show that vision to others? We are his witnesses; how do others see that witness in us? Whatever the occasion, do we display appropriate Christian witness or are we, like fashions in clothes, always trimming our Christian behaviour.

THIRTEENTH SUNDAY AFTER PENTECOST

Appropriate attitudes

St Matthew 10.16 (NEB) *'Look I send you out.'*

INTRODUCTION

Jesus invited the inner band of apostles to follow him, sharing in his ministry as far as they could. At the same time he was preparing them for their future apostolic ministry. They had been chosen; now they were being sent out and Jesus told them of the task they were to perform, the reception they were likely to experience and the attitude they should adopt in these circumstances.

APPLICATION

How appropriate are those instructions today?

Like sheep among wolves

The apostolic experience was of persecution, suffering and martyrdom. Although some Christians are persecuted today, this is not our experience in Britain. Neverthless we are attacked for our Christian witness. A bishop or a priest may be attacked for having spoken out on an issue; or even for having kept silent. The Church as a whole may be attacked. Jesus suffered; and as his followers we can expect to suffer for our faith. This may often be mental or spiritual suffering; we are ridiculed for holding apparently naive beliefs.

Be wary as serpents

Surely Jesus is not intending us to follow the wiles of the devil to protect ourselves? No, Jesus is telling us to be wary and to protect our faith, as a serpent slithers away from threatening danger. Our faith is to be protected to allow it to grow, no matter how adverse the circumstances.

Innocent as doves

Innocency can be assumed or phoney. The kind of innocency which Jesus asks his disciples to display is innocency of the life of the Spirit. Do you remember how at his baptism the Holy Spirit descended upon our Lord in the form and appearance of a dove. Pureness of living is required of the Christian disciple.

Be on your guard

Not to protect yourself from the consequences of your Christian witness, but to be sure always to witness faithfully by word and deed.

Do not worry

This is perhaps the most needful to heed. All of us worry, worry, worry. We assume that all problems must be solved by us. We need to remember that God cares for each one of us. It is God's world; he is supreme and all is well!

All will hate you

In a post-Christian Britain nearly all people have some knowledge of Jesus. They may even have a commitment of a kind. Many hate to be reminded of this by our faithful witness as practising, worshipping Christians. It may well be true that many find the worship of the church unintelligible or irrelevant; does not our perseverance cause them to 'hate us'?

The man who holds out to the end will be saved

All men are saved through the crucified, risen and ascended Lord. All need to claim that benefit through penitence, thanksgiving and service, persevering to the end.

FOURTEENTH SUNDAY AFTER PENTECOST

It's all there!

St Luke 16.31 (NEB) *'If they do not listen to Moses and the prophets they will pay no heed even if someone should rise from the dead.'*

INTRODUCTION

There were six brothers brought up in complete luxury and comfort; the sons of a rich man. They had all they wanted and gave dinner parties almost daily to which they invited their many friends. Living in such luxury they did not think much about the future, and their religious beliefs as Saduccees made them doubtful of any general resurrection. They lived for the present. One of the brothers, Dives, died, and to his surprise found himself in Hades. Even there his character had not changed. He had been so accustomed to ordering people about that he demanded of Abraham that he send Lazarus 'to dip his finger in water to cool his tongue' for he was suffering torment in the heat of the fire. He still thought of himself first. It was not until his request was firmly refused that he thought of others; then he thought not of Lazarus but of his five remaining brothers. He knew the kind of life they would still be leading on earth; they would be 'living it up' without any thought for tomorrow or anybody else. 'At least,' Dives thought, 'I can perhaps save them from this agony.' Could they not be warned by Lazarus? Could not the poor beggar be sent as a ghost to warn this tough family of brothers who had no fear of God or man? Dives knew his brothers were superstitious and if they were haunted by the ghost of someone they knew but never cared for, this might bring about a change of heart. Abraham replied, 'If they do not listen to Moses and the prophets they will pay no need even if someone should rise from the dead.' How true! Jesus rose from the dead; and countless men and women in all centuries since then have paid no need to our risen and ascended Lord.

What is the meaning of this parable? It is not a commentary on social and class distinctions, other than to remind us that all men are equal in the sight of God. Nor does it illustrate how selfishness and self-indulgence in this life will be punished; Jesus was not emphasising a doctrine of rewards and punishments and he gave no indication of the kind of life that Lazarus led other than that he was poor. He was primarily concerned with the response of Dives to the religious opportunities he had been given and only secondarily with his use of wealth to do good. The six brothers professed obedience to the teachings of Moses and the prophets, yet they were blind to the real meaning of the scriptures.

APPLICATION

We need to look at our Bible again and see what God is trying to tell us in the law and the prophets and through the fuller revelation of Jesus, who did rise from the dead. It's all there! There is a growing concern that the new literate peoples of the world should feed their minds on Christ. What about you? What about a local challenge? Feed the soul through the mind. The scriptures are the appointed means of grace, why don't we use them? We cannot earn our way to heaven; but we can seek to know and obey the will of God, no matter what is our station in life.

FIFTEENTH SUNDAY AFTER PENTECOST

Cost of living

St Luke 14.33 (NEB) 'None of you can be a disciple of mine without parting with all his possessions.'

INTRODUCTION

'The cost of living index rose by three points last month'. This announcement comes as no surprise to the observant housewife as she regularly shops. She is surprised at the very small increase in the index, as in her own experience food prices seem to have risen by leaps and bounds.

How does the housewife meet this problem of inflation? By using time and energy looking for bargains or special-price offers and by comparing prices. The weekly budget may be very tight, and at home she discusses the problem with her husband. How does the wage-earner meet the problem of rising prices? His trade union may succeed in negotiating a new wage settlement; but the only time he feels rich is when he receives back pay and even then the tax man appears to take most of it. Often the only immediate answer is to work overtime or to take a spare-time job, or for his wife to take up paid employment.

Is the young executive or professional man in a different position? He may try to guard against inflation by buying his own house; but the monthly mortgage payments are so high, insurance and rates adding to the expenditure; so that again there is no alternative to his wife doing a job. It is possible that the wife herself is professionally trained and anxious to pursue her career and so they may decide not to have a family.

And all this is done to maintain a standard of living to which they have been accustomed. This is the cost of human existence in technological Britain. But is it *real* living? Where in all this can we discern a man or woman growing in stature into their real selves, made in the image of God? Small wonder that Jesus said: 'None of you can be a disciple of mine without parting with all his possessions.' This was not addressed to the inner band of apostles who had given up all and followed him. It was said to the crowd who followed him enthusiastically on his way to Jerusalem. It is not addressed today to those in the ordained ministry only, but to all Christians and means: 'Get your priorities right'. Possessions, even the possession of a family, can be a hindrance to committed discipleship.

APPLICATION

What is the cost of living for Christian discipleship? It means the giving up of whole life to him and perhaps we can test our willingness to embrace the way of disciples by answering the following questions. What time each Sunday do I give to the worship of God? Is a communion once a month really enough? Do I say my prayers daily? What time am I prepared to give in direct service to the Church's evangelisation and mission? Are we prepared to meet the cost of living the way of Christ? It is the Way of the Cross.

SIXTEENTH SUNDAY AFTER PENTECOST

A parish prayer

St Luke 11.1 (NEB) '*Teach us to pray.*'

INTRODUCTION

When Jesus rose from praying the disciples asked him to 'teach us to pray'. They were not without some knowledge of prayer as they were accustomed to services in the synagogue and in the temple. Although the request was made by an individual disciple it was to meet a corporate need. '*Teach us to pray*'. Every priest is asked for help in prayer and there are many ways in which help can be given. Today I want to give one way; it may help to achieve a new dimension and depth in the corporate prayer of this parish.

APPLICATION

A small group of representatives of my parish spent a residential weekend together, the third annual conference we had held. In the course of the discussion it was suggested that there was a need for a parish prayer. On our return the parish liturgical committee (under the guidance of our junior curate) gave long and serious consideration to this request. Almost a year later on Trinity Sunday 1972 the prayer was introduced at our Sunday services. Prayer cards had been printed and we asked our congregation to take them home and use them daily at 11 a.m. and 4 p.m.; the hour at which we began our daily offices in church.

Thus, for a brief half minute, there would be a wave of corporate prayer offered by Holy Trinity worshippers, whereever we might be; making our fellowship in prayer more real. Here is the prayer we introduced; there is no copyright, but it would be better if you produced your own parish prayer.

> HOLY TRINITY
> in whose name we worship,
> give us such love, that,
> alone and together, today and everyday,
> we may reverence the Father,
> radiate the presence of the Son,
> and live in the power of the Holy Spirit. Amen.*

Holy Trinity

Jesus taught his disciples to address God in a way different to the Jewish custom. Any Jew could have prayed 'Our Father who art in heaven' using the formal and exclusively religious *Abinu*. Jesus used the word '*Abba*' thus transferring the Fatherhood of God from a theological doctrine into an intense and intimate experience. In our parish prayer we have sought to make the Holy Trinity an experience of prayer and life; we pray in the name of God who created us, Christ who redeemed us and the Holy Spirit who sanctifies us.

Give us such love

There was a great debate to get something about love into the prayer as love of God and love of each other is essential to Christian fellowship; and you know how difficult it is to have *agape* even in a church.

Alone and together

This is a deliberate phrase. One member may be physically alone, perhaps at the kitchen sink when she says this prayer; but there is a deeper truth that as part of the fellowship we can never be alone.

*The daily prayer of the Parish of Holy Trinity, Northwood, London.

Reverence the Father

Hallowing God's name. Radiate the presence of the Son, being Christ-like. Live in the power of the Holy Spirit. Only in this power can we come closer to Christian perfection.

'Teach us to pray'

What about a parish prayer for this parish?

SEVENTEENTH SUNDAY AFTER PENTECOST

Response to Christ's authority

> St Luke 7.3 (NEB) *'Hearing about Jesus, he sent some Jewish elders with a request that he would come and save his servant's life.'*

Occasionally in a novel or play the principal character never appears, and yet we are not unaware of the absent character's vital part in the whole story. In today's gospel we cannot be unaware of the influential part played by the centurion whom we never meet. And yet we feel we know a lot about this army officer and learn through him about Christ's authority to which he responded in faith.

Our centurion was a man who exercised authority, expecting immediate response to his commands, 'Go', 'Come here', 'Do this'. He also knew that obedience to his commands depended upon the source of his authority which was independent of him, his commission from Herod Antipas in whose service he was enlisted. The centurion had never met Jesus, he had only heard about him, what he had said and what he had done and that he acted with authority. The centurion recognised that Jesus' authority came not from himself but from some higher source; we know that authority to have come from God.

Nowadays authority is questioned and challenged and is unacceptable to some. It is claimed that a man must earn respect rather than claim it by an office he holds. There is some justice in this. All who are in positions of authority ought to act in accordance with the trust placed in them. Nevertheless there is one area in life where authority needs to be recognised; the authority given to the Church by Christ; not to acknowledge that authority is to deny the authority of Jesus. The authority for celebrating this eucharist is Christ, who said 'Do this in remembrance of me'. Jesus has provided a priesthood with authority to absolve sinners in his name; and all men are sinners. Do you recognise the authority of Jesus?

The centurion showed compassion. He had power as an army officer and could command obedience. Yet when one of his servants was ill, whom he valued highly, he sent for Jesus to come and save him. We admire the compassion of Jesus; do we emulate him?

The centurion was not a Jew. However, he had come to admire the religious qualities of Judaism although he had not become a proselyte. He remained a gentile, but he nevertheless built a synagogue for the people of Capernaum, and it was the elders of this synagogue who approached Jesus on his behalf. The centurion knew the rules which governed Jewish relations with gentiles and he was not prepared to put Jesus in an invidious position by asking him to come to his home. But Jesus in his love and compassion was too strong to be bound by restrictive custom and was, no doubt, prepared to come to the house. However, he saw the quality of the life of the centurion and his faith, so he made no attempt to see his servant. When the messengers returned to the centurion's house they found the servant restored to good health. Jesus comes to us in this eucharist to make us whole again, unworthy though we be to receive him. How strong is our faith?

EIGHTEENTH SUNDAY AFTER PENTECOST

Capital achievement

St Matthew 25.14 (NEB) *'It is like a man going abroad, who called his servants and put his capital in their hands.'*

INTRODUCTION

Hilary eagerly ripped open the telegram she had been expecting from her son Giles. It read: 'GOT A FIRST CLASS—GILES.' This was excellent news and meant that Giles could take up the industrial research appointment which he had been offered conditional upon his obtaining a good class in his engineering degree at Southampton. At once Hilary rang up John at his office to tell him of their son's success.

That Thursday seemed to be a long one for Hilary as she got on with her housework; she longed for John to come home so that they could share their joy in Giles' success. She was no less busy than usual, but she thought she would occupy the time by preparing a special evening meal. Punctually at half-past six she heard the tyres of John's car as he drove up the gravelled drive; she knew he was home before he sounded his customary hoot to announce his arrival.

Soon they were sitting down to their meal and John opened a bottle of wine, so that they might suitably toast their son and his success. But somehow the dinner did not turn out as planned by Hilary. The food and the wine were excellent. They were both elated at Giles' achievement and were delighted that he had successfully launched his career.

But they could not forget Andrew, the older brother, for whom they felt the same love. He possessed greater intellectual powers than Giles and from the same grammar school he had won an open scholarship to Oxford. There he had met a girl and Andrew had given more of his time to her than to his studies. At the end of his first year he had been sent down. The girl became pregnant, and somewhere or other they were now living together as hippies. What a waste of talent!

John and Hilary also had a daughter, Rosemary, who did not possess the same academic ability as her brothers. Fortunately for her, the local authority had switched to comprehensives by the time she had reached secondary school. Here she had soon discovered that her gifts were artistic. Now she was launched on her chosen career as an apprentice-hairdresser.

APPLICATION

It does not matter what talents we possess, we all have some. It matters that we use them to the full and use them purposefully. Jesus is not unlike the man who went abroad in the parable; he has returned to his Father and left the furtherance of his kingdom for us to share in as his servants. How shall we use the capital opportunity given to each one of us?

NINETEENTH SUNDAY AFTER PENTECOST

Guest of a sinner

St Luke 19.7 (NEB) *'He has gone in, they said, to be the guest of a sinner.'*

INTRODUCTION

Do you like the tax man? Very few of us have ever met one, except perhaps to discuss our tax position with an inland revenue officer across the counter at the tax office. Even then it is not likely that we know his name, and unless there is an inland revenue officer among our circle of friends we probably know nothing about the tax man personally. Our reaction to the tax inspector is that we dislike having to part with any of our income. If this is the common attitude today, when any one of us can know the rates of taxation payable, allowances that we can claim, and the purposes for which the revenue is required, what was the attitude towards Zaccheaus the rich tax-gatherer contemporary of Jesus of Nazareth?

Then, as now, governments needed money. Often the need

was immediate and there was not enough time for the tax to be collected from all those liable to pay. The government farmed taxes out in return for immediate capital. Although we are not fully conversant with Zaccheus' tax situation it is probable that he acted in this way for the imperial power of Rome. He was superintendent of taxes and a very rich man. His job made him a social outcast and he was ostracised. Small in stature he was anxious to see Jesus; his social relationship to his contemporaries made it impossible for him to seek their help in getting to the front of the crowd. Determined not to be defeated Zaccheus ran ahead of the crowd and climbed a tree so that he might see Jesus as he passed by. When he took this action he could not have contemplated what the outcome would be. Jesus asked if he might stay with Zaccheus where his normal experience, was that others avoided his friendship. Zaccheus' encounter with Jesus proved costly: he was willing to give half of his possessions to charity and what is more, if he had cheated anyone on tax assessment he would repay him fourfold. This was the man whom contemporaries called a sinner; 'he has gone in to be the guest of a sinner'. They did not know the man; what is more they did not consider themselves to be sinners.

APPLICATION

Today's gospel reminds us that Jesus comes to each one of us as sinners. This encounter will be costly for us; it means that confronted by the love of God we must disown our sinful nature. We must willingly give up all sins which militate against our love of God. We have a pretty good idea of where we fall short. And yet to all sinners Jesus says, 'I must come and stay with you today.' (St Luke 19.5). Should we not earnestly pray, 'Come lord, stay with me always'?

TWENTIETH SUNDAY AFTER PENTECOST

Prepared for the crisis?

St Matthew 25.1 (NEB) *'When that day comes.'*

INTRODUCTION

Wedding customs vary from country to country and in the course of history as social patterns change. Today there are some in England who claim that marriage is out-of-date. If we are to understand the parable which Jesus told about the waiting bridesmaids we must recognise the Jewish marriage customs of those days. This will answer two questions which you may have asked: why did the bridegroom not know the five bridesmaids when they arrived at the door, and why, in the first instance, were the bridesmaids not with the bride, as we would expect them to be? In a Jewish wedding it was customary for the bridegroom, along with his friends, to come to the bride's home and take her to his home for the ceremony. The bridesmaids would attend the bridegroom when he did so. The bridesmaids were the bride's friends and it is quite possible for the bridegroom not to know them, especially if the marriage had been arranged or was between a couple who did not live in the same town or region. The bridesmaids were playing their customary part and we should expect them all to be fully conversant with the arrangements, to equip themselves fully for their role. Jesus said that five were ready and five unprepared.

What is the significance of this parable? We must first try to answer another question: 'To whom did Jesus tell this story?' It might well have been told to the religious leaders of his day, who were unprepared for the coming of the Messiah. The disciples would also have heard the story and it had also a message for them; be ready for each testing time, the crisis situation in which you make a judgement to act as a follower of mine and on how you act you will be judged by God. Matthew, who was crisis-conscious particularly over the second coming of Christ, puts the parable in the context of the final crisis, the

Last Judgement. When that day comes and the Kingdom of Heaven is realised in accord with God's fulfilling there will be a judgement; be prepared.

APPLICATION

Although the full realisation of the kingdom will be in God's good time, the kingdom is already in existence and as Christians committed to work for its establishment we encounter many crisis times in our lives when we need to make a judgement. Reflect on how Peter denied Jesus, Judas betrayed him and his disciples deserted him and fled. How prepared are we for each crisis when a Christian judgement is necessary? Do we turn it into a Christus-time allowing God to rule our hearts and judgements?

TWENTY-FIRST SUNDAY AFTER PENTECOST

One way only

St Matthew 7.13–14 (NEB) '*Enter by the narrow gate . . . the gate that leads to life is small and the road is narrow, and those who find it are few.*'

INTRODUCTION

'One way only'; any driver seeing such a traffic sign knows instantly its implications, that although the way ahead is clear, to ignore the sign and go contrary to the traffic flow is to invite, if not to cause disaster. Jesus said that the wide road of life which so many follow leads to disaster and that the one way of life to follow is through the narrow gate and by the narrow road.

Why then do so many find the narrow way so unattractive? Because they believe the Christian way to be restrictive and there is a great deal of puritanical expression of religion to give grounds for such an understanding. There are some contemporary Christian writers, on the other hand, who believe that twentieth-century man has come of age and a sort of 'religion-less-Christianity' is what he needs. They welcome the permissive society which, they say, gives man a freedom consistent with the Gospel. We need to emphasise that the narrow way is a releasing experience and not a restricting one.

The way is narrow because there is only one objective: to know and to serve God. There is only one way to begin the journey and that is through Jesus Christ our Lord. For most of us that journey begins at the font, though some see a conversion experience as essential. Once through the narrow gate of accepting Christ as our Lord and Master, there remains the narrow road to follow. But we can get lost or misled. On life's journey, we shall find many voices urging us to do this or that as Christians. Many people find it confusing and disturbing that the Church does not speak with a united voice on many contemporary issues. On the journey there are two warnings to be observed; we are to beware of false prophets and we must take care that we are not ourselves false prophets. True prophets can be recognised by the fruits of the spirit.

APPLICATION

Once embarked on the Christian journey we are all prophets, proclaiming the way of the Lord in word and deed although only a few exercise a prophetic ministry in terms of preaching. Are we true or false prophets? We may, for instance, adopt a modern outlook and claim that a permissive society is nearest to the Christian ideal for it enables a free man to become truly human and reach towards that image of God which Christians believe to be man's true nature. The permissive opportunity to be truly human in response to divine will is one thing; but to use that freedom to follow uninhibited desires is to stray on to the broad way of life which leads to destruction. Are we true or false prophets? Only the extent to which we remain loyal and faithful to our Lord provides the answer. It is how we live as Christians which matters, not only for our own well-being but for others for we are all prophets whether we like it or not. Shall we be true or false?

TWENTY-SECOND SUNDAY AFTER PENTECOST

Worship

St Mark 2.27 (NEB) *'The Sabbath was made for the sake of man and not man for the Sabbath: therefore the Son of Man is sovereign over the Sabbath.'*

INTRODUCTION

Jesus made it clear that the Sabbath is made for the sake of man. What about Sunday observance? As Christians we have a witness to bear without imposing puritanical restraints on ourselves or others. Our essential witness is in our churchgoing; but why come to Church?

APPLICATION

Weekly

Each Sunday we acknowledge that Christ is sovereign and in our eucharist celebrate his mighty Resurrection (that is why we keep the first day of the week and not the seventh). Do we make this a weekly obligation, giving true significance to Sunday or does our worship take its place alongside alternative priorities—gardening to be done or the cars to be washed?

Offer

We come to offer ourselves, our work and our leisure. The weekly round is offered to Christ, the eucharistic bread and wine reminding us of our labour and leisure. We pray to be sent out into the world in the power of the Holy Spirit and now we bring our imperfect offering to Christ.

Repent

When we recollect the imperfection of our offering during the past week we are aware that we have not always done our best leaving things undone which we ought to have tackled. There is always the imperfect way in which we have done things.

Sometimes we have denied our Christian way of life. So corporately and individually we need to repent, to confess our sins as we do in this service as people preparing to meet their Lord.

Sing

Choirs and congregations enjoy singing, although the enjoyment is not always so evident as it ought to be. Hymns, psalms and music are essential parts of our worship. Like David we sing unto the Lord; like Jesus and his disciples we sing.

Hear

Jesus tells us to listen with perception. How do we listen to the readings? How attentive are we to the Word which is preached? The reading of the lessons and the preaching of the sermon are not solo turns; they are corporate acts in which the Holy Spirit is active.

Intercession

Prayer is of the essence of Christian worship; together we pray for others and ourselves.

Praise

The purpose of our worship is to praise Almighty God for whom he is—creator, redeemer and sanctifier. We reflect on his glory and respond in praise; and offer thanksgiving for what he has done for us.

Why come to Church

WORSHIP is the answer and the initial letters of this word remind us to come *weekly* to *offer* ourselves, *repent* our sins, *sing* our hymns, *hear* his most holy Word, offer *intercession* for all and to *praise* and thank our God.

TWENTY-THIRD SUNDAY
AFTER PENTECOST

There's a time and a place

St Mark 2.18 (NEB) '*Why is it that John's disciples and the disciples of the Pharisees are fasting, but yours are not?*'

INTRODUCTION

We should not be surprised that this question was asked of Jesus, 'Why is it that John's disciples and the disciples of the Pharisees are fasting and yours are not?' Fasting was part of Jewish religious observance and those who were eagerly preparing for the kingdom were careful to observe this practice. Jesus, you will recall, fasted forty days in the wilderness before he actively engaged in proclaiming the kingdom of God. John the Baptist was noted, even criticised, for his austerity; and in today's gospel we are informed that his disciples were fasting. The Jews sometimes observed a fast as a sign of mourning and it has been suggested by some commentators that John's disciples were in fact mourning his death. But this does not account for the fact that disciples of the Pharisees were fasting at this same period. Why then were the disciples of Jesus not fasting? Surely the followers of so authoritative a leader as Jesus was recognised to be should also be fasting?

Jesus does not say that they should not fast; he says that there is a time and a place for fasting as there is also a time and a place for rejoicing. These are separate though related acts; never to be mixed without courting disaster. 'No one sews a patch of unshrunk cloth on to an old coat' (St Mark 2.21). 'No one puts new wine into old wine-skins' (St Mark 2.22). There is a time and a place and Jesus identifies appropriate action with the presence of the bridegroom.

APPLICATION

At each eucharist we are in the presence of the bridegroom and it is therefore a time for rejoicing and thanksgiving. How then can any Christian limit the number of times in a year that he comes into the eucharistic presence and makes his communion? Should we not all be in the Lord's house on the Lord's day for the Lord's own service? The reason which some people give for a less frequent making of their communion is that they need to come prepared. Indeed we should all come prepared and this is where fasting has a time and a place in our preparation. Most people if asked, 'What is fasting?', would reply 'Eating fish on Fridays', for this is the popular understanding of its meaning. But this is abstinence, the giving up of something like meat on Fridays or sugar during Lent.

To fast is to give up food and drink entirely or to restrict yourself to one main meal a day. People anxious to slim often do this, but that does not make it fasting. Fasting is a deliberate attempt to weaken our desires for sensible pleasures as a means of liberating and strengthening our spiritual lives. In the teaching of Jesus it is accompanied by prayer. There is a time and a place for fasting and it should not be limited to the Lenten season or some demonstration of intention during Christian Aid week. It may well be that we have much to learn from Eastern religions of the place of a definite and periodic scaling down of our physical needs in order to sharpen our spiritual armour.

NINTH SUNDAY BEFORE CHRISTMAS

Listen to the wind

> St John 3.8 (NEB) '*The wind blows where it wills; you hear the sound of it, but you do not know where it comes from, or where it is going. So with everyone who is born from spirit.*'

INTRODUCTION

Two men were completely immersed in conversation. It was evening. As they sat upon the hillside the wind blew through the trees bringing refreshing coolness after the heat of the day.

If anyone else had seen them, as they earnestly discussed the meaning of life, they might have questioned what brought them together under cover of darkness; a respected representative of the establishment talking with the severest critic of authority. Nicodemus knew that if he was seen, his action might be mis-construed. That is why he went by night to see Jesus—to avoid detection. He could not resist the opportunity to explore the discerning mind of Christ. It was Nicodemus' search for truth that brought him into dialogue with Jesus.

Both were knowledgeable in the scriptures. Nicodemus was a theologian of some standing. Jesus is the Word of God. Jesus directed Nicodemus that night to the need for a man to be born again of the Spirit if he is to see the kingdom of God (St John 3.3). 'But how is this possible?' Nicodemus asked. 'Listen to the wind, Nicodemus, listen to the wind'. Jesus used this illustration to indicate the dynamic power of the Holy Spirit.

APPLICATION

Consider the power of the wind as you drive through the countryside of East Anglia where the bent trees indicate the direction of the prevailing wind. The Holy Spirit seeks to shape the lives of men in accordance with God's Will. Where is the evidence of the prevailing dynamic Spirit today? There are some who find it in contemporary religious movements which are critical of the institutional church, as Jesus was critical of institutional religion in Jerusalem. This is not to say that the dynamic Spirit is inactive in the Church today; the evidence is to the contrary. Reflect on the tremendous change in attitude and worship in the Roman Catholic church since Pope John. The problem is that we tend to protect ourselves from the disturbing influence of the Spirit, just as we try to shield our-selves from the wind. Such attempts are in vain and should be abandoned, that was what Jesus was saying to Nicodemus and he is saying the same to us today. Leave yourself open to the Spirit.

We are renewed by baptism of the Spirit; this is the releasing experience of utter response to the Spirit who creates cosmos out of chaos; this we learn from the Hebrew understanding of the Creation. In that creative activity God encourages us to share. The Spirit creating cosmos out of chaos—like the wind—destroys that which needs purging, offers refreshment (like the wind in the heat of the day) and is dynamic in its purpose.

EIGHTH SUNDAY BEFORE CHRISTMAS

Food for thought

St Mark 7.15 (NEB) *'Nothing that goes into a man from outside can defile him; no, it is the things that come out of him that defile a man.'*

INTRODUCTION

Are you calorie conscious? Women's magazines, newspaper features and commercial advertising encourage us to be calorie conscious for two principal reasons: that we may avoid the dangers of overweight and be more attractive in appearance—fat conscious and figure conscious. Although dieting may add something to our energy and enjoyment of life, it in no way adds to the quality of living.

The dietary regulations in Jewish society were considered to possess a moral function; to break them could make a person unclean and in a wrong relationship to God. For example in 'coming from the market-place they never eat without first washing' (St Mark 7.3). Surely we would commend such an hygienic practice. But it was not hygiene which governed this practice. The Jews washed their hands as a sign that they were God's chosen people. On the way from the market-place they might have been touched (even accidentally) by a Gentile and this they believed made them unclean in God's sight until they had washed their hands.

Jesus taught that you may have clean hands, though this does not mean that your hearts are clean in God's sight. Indeed what we see and hear may defile us; more than bacteria from unwashed hands. St Mark presents us with a parable of Jesus in one sentence—'Nothing that goes into a man from outside can defile him; no, it is the things which come out of him that defile a man'—the understanding of which depends upon possessing the key. Verses seventeen to twenty-three gave the unfolding of its meaning to the disciples.

APPLICATION

Although it is true that physical fitness aids our mental alertness and assists our spiritual growth, we cannot deny that it is how we think and act that determines the quality of human living. For Christians an approximation to the life of Christ is the desirable norm. The elucidation of the parable is concerned with what may defile a man or increase his potential to evil. 'For from inside out of a man's heart' (St Mark 7.21) comes evil. In these days of heart transplants and greater awareness of coronary illnesses, we are perhaps more aware than ever of the heart as the vital source of life.

It was in the sense of the heart as the source of life that Jesus spoke of that which comes out of a man's heart as the source of evil and good. We attribute emotions to the heart. Valentine cards carry a heart design to indicate love for someone. It is from our own wilful determination and not from what we eat that evil intentions emerge. Evil thoughts father evil acts. Evil acts defile us and make us evil persons—this is what Jesus was saying.

SEVENTH SUNDAY BEFORE CHRISTMAS

Labourers in the vineyard

St Luke 20.9 (NEB) *'A man planted a vineyard, let it out to vinegrowers.'*

INTRODUCTION

Those who heard the parable of the vineyard owner and his tenants were well able to picture the situation. The owner had planted the vineyard, but there was quite a time before the vines matured to produce the grapes or olives. During that period the tenants had carefully cultivated the vines and their attitude when the agent called for the owner's share is not difficult to imagine. 'Why should he have so great a percentage? Without our labour and care there would be no crop. Capitalist! What has he really done to deserve this share; he was fortunate enough to possess the land and have some means.' Three agents came and were successively treated more outrageously. When the son was sent they disposed of him outside the vineyard. With the sole heir out of the way, they had a better chance of getting possession as sitting-tenants should anything untoward happen to the owner. Having told the story Jesus posed the question, 'What then will the owner of the vineyard do to them?' and he proceeded to give the answer, 'He will come and put these tenants to death and let the vineyard to others' (St Luke 20.15, 16). Not an unexpected answer but how is this parable to be understood?

How did the Jews understand this parable?

We can only answer this question if we recognise that there is in the story an allusion to a prophetic passage in Isaiah, which the Jewish hearers would grasp immediately: 'The vineyard of the Lord of Hosts is Israel' (Isaiah 5.7). The parable was concerned with the dealing of God with his people. The Jews' immediate reaction was to reject the implications of the story that the landlord was God, the tenants were the rulers (civil and ecclesiastical), the agents were the prophets who had been consistently disregarded and persecuted. Their outspoken opposition—'God forbid' (St Luke 20.16) referred principally to the concluding part of the parable. They also found unacceptable the implication of the Messiahship of Jesus, and rejected the possibility that they would lose their inheritance and this would be given to the Gentiles.

How did the early Churches interpret the parable?

God was the landlord, the Jewish authorities were the rebellious tenants, the prophets were the agents of God and Jesus was the beloved son finally sent, who they flung out of the vineyard and killed. This was interpreted as foretelling Christ's death outside the city of Jerusalem, and under the new covenant, Christians became the new tenants.

APPLICATION

We are the tenants of the vineyard in our own generation. Do we question the authority of God as creator? Do we recognise those whom God has sent and sends to interpret his purposes for us? Above all, do we recognise the person and mission of Jesus? Finally, are we labourers worthy of our tenancy?

SIXTH SUNDAY BEFORE CHRISTMAS

All is well

St Mark 13.13 (NEB) '*All will hate you for your allegiance to me; but the man who holds out to the end will be saved.*'

INTRODUCTION

This generation is perhaps more aware than any previous generation of catastrophes, accidents and disasters. Press, radio and television bring us instant coverage; be it a plane disaster in Brazil, a coup in Ghana, an earthquake in Persia, warfare in the Middle East, civil unrest in America or Northern Ireland, famine in India and Pakistan. The range of our awareness is increased, but there is nothing new in human experience of disasters, natural and man-motivated. Such experiences were not uncommon for first century Christians. There were wars and rumours of wars on the eastern frontiers of the Roman empire; there were risings in Palestine. When Claudius and Nero were emperors, we know of famines and earthquakes. Then, as now, people asked why should this be and some, familiar with the Old Testament, might claim; 'this is the beginning of the end'.

Jesus warns of certain disastrous events. The truth of that warning is confirmed by the continuance of like disasters twenty centuries later. Jesus gives specific warnings to Christians: they will be brought to trial now, as in the first century; they will be punished for their faith; they will be betrayed; there will be division in families, because of allegiance to Christ. How true, then and now! But the warnings were given with the assurance that all is well for 'the man who holds out to the end will be saved'. (St Mark 13.13). The important thing is to keep a firm hold on one's faith and not to be agitated or overcome by the disasters of life. If we endure in the faith, all is well. We are not left to struggle on our own.

APPLICATION

'With these things the birthpangs of the new age begins.' The new age has begun, but we still labour in bringing it to fullness in and with Christ. As Michael Quoist so ably expresses this:

> 'Man can live the Creation, the Incarnation, the Redemption, and the Resurrection in every one of his acts. He can live the Creation because by the very act of living, he is completing his own creation and, in the company of his brothers, that of the world. He can live the Incarnation because, by accepting with love the presence of Jesus Christ, he allows Christ to take him over completely. He can live the Redemption since, because of sin, there is not a second of his life that does not necessitate struggle, suffering, and death to himself. If it is lived with Christ, that battle against selfishness, pride, and non-love can only lead to the victory of the Resurrection, by virtue of which that particle of life enters into Life—into true life, which is eternal.
>
> 'Thus, the Christian who, through faith, discovers Christ living in the centre of life can join Christ and live out the Mystery of Christ with him. But he can also reject the encounter and union with Christ. He must therefore acquire the spiritual habit, as it were, of that encounter, through loyalty with respect to living his faith in his life. Just as he must go beyond the words

of the Evangelists if he is to find Christ in the Gospel, so too must he go beyond life's events in order to find life itself'.*

In that living we shall find that men hate us for our allegiance to Christ, 'but the man who holds out to the end will be saved'.

FIFTH SUNDAY BEFORE CHRISTMAS

Ever watchful

St Mark 13.23 (NEB) *'But you be on your guard.'*

INTRODUCTION

Have you ever tried to read the last book in the Bible—*The Revelation of John*? If so, what did you make of it? Certainly it reminds us that the Bible is a library of books. It is a specialist library, because the compilers have only included books which they thought threw light on a particular subject—the Testament or Covenant. *The Revelation of John* is an apocalyptic writing, a vision of the final cosmic drama which God would initiate. The basic pattern is a period of intensified tribulation, followed by the judgement, the new age, and the reward of the righteous; the catastrophes foretold supernatural upheavals with conflict between cosmic and mythological powers. This Christian apocalypse is intended to encourage us; the climax is the establishment of a new order by God when at last his chosen people will take their rightful place.

What has all this to do with today's gospel reading? In the first verse which we read (St Mark 13.14) there occurs a curious sentence in parentheses: '(let the reader understand)'. 'Let the reader understand' suggests that at some stage before the gospel was written, a saying of Jesus had been assimilated to the conventions of a written apocalypse. But the 'little apocalypse' of St Mark chapter thirteen (as it is so often called) differs from the apocalyptic *Revelation of John*. Whereas in *The Revelation* we get a poetic presentation of events and tribulations far

*Michael Quoist: *Christ is Alive!* English edition, Gill and Macmillan, Dublin, 1971. pp. 123, 124. (Reproduced by permission of the publisher).

removed from life, Jesus' discourse was set firmly within history: the writing of this part of Mark's gospel may have been influenced by an event which took place in AD 40. In that year the Roman Emperor attempted to have a statue of himself placed in the temple at Jerusalem, 'Usurping a place which was not his' (St Mark 13.14).

Commentators on this passage are not agreed on all details of interpretation and exegesis. We need only to remember that this passage came out of Jewish and Christian experience (where it was necessary to give encouragement to Christians in their trials and tribulations) that God 'for the sake of his own, whom he has chosen, he has cut short the time' of trials (St Mark 13.20). The important point is not the scene or the occasion of its fulfilment, it is the warning of Jesus: *'But you be on your guard'*.

APPLICATION

Attacks on Jerusalem were recurrent experiences and in the first century AD the Temple was indeed destroyed. *'Then those who are in Judaea must take to the hills'* (St Mark 13.14), was practical advice, flight to the hill places and caves where the invading armies would not follow. Will there be time? There will not even be time for a man working on the roof of his house to come down the outdoor stairway and enter the house to collect things. It will be even more difficult if the attack comes in the winter when travel on roads ruined by rain will be more hazardous. *'But you, be on your guard'* (St Mark 13.23). Christians of the first century would see the significance of this warning against the background of contemporary events; but there was an additional reason for Mark including it in this 'little apocalypse'. It had been expected that Jesus would return in glory in a very short time and that expectation had not been fulfilled. This had not led to disbelief, but to unpreparedness and relaxation.

Our Christian commitment is not carried out in fear of invasion and trials. There is nevertheless a danger that we may not be on our guard against more subtle ways of attack. Today Jesus says to us, 'Be on your guard; I have forewarned you of it all'. To be forewarned is to be forearmed. Are we ever watchful?